YOGA AND WESTERN PSYCHOLOGY

YOGA
AND WESTERN
PSYCHOLOGY
A COMPARISON

By

GERALDINE COSTER
Author of PSYCHO-ANALYSIS FOR
NORMAL PEOPLE

HARPER COLOPHON BOOKS

Harper & Row, Publishers

New York, Evanston, San Francisco, London

YOGA AND WESTERN PSYCHOLOGY

First HARPER COLOPHON EDITION published in 1972

STANDARD BOOK NUMBER: 06-091007-0

PREFACE TO THE PAPERBACK EDITION

SINCE *this book was originally published in 1934, many changes have taken place in psychology, but the problems that the author dealt with remain the same today (only more so) so her books cannot be said to have dated. Human nature stays much as it always has been, and the search for truth follows differing paths from time to time. In spite of the enormous increase in western knowledge people remain just as ignorant about "what the will is, or how it works," and similar problems, the solution of which can only be reached through self-knowledge acquired by the practice of a reliable method.*

The only omission from the original book is a diagram (which the author owed to Mrs. E. L. Gardner) and the references to it in chapter XV. In the light of subsequent advances in all the biological sciences, this diagram can serve no useful purpose nowadays.

Marion Cardew

London, 1971

ACKNOWLEDGMENTS

FORMAL *acknowledgments are inadequate to express the debt that this book owes to my friends Mrs. E. L. Gardner and Miss Margaret Lee. The paraphrase of the Yoga Sutras in Chapter VII was worked out in close collaboration with Mrs. Gardner and owes much to her knowledge and insight. Miss Lee has once more given generously of her valuable time and her special skill to the labour of revision and proof-correcting, and for this thankless task she has my heartfelt thanks*

G. C.

WYCHWOOD SCHOOL,
OXFORD

CONTENTS

Part I. ANALYTICAL THERAPY

Part II. YOGA

Part III. A COMPARISON

ANALYTICAL THERAPY

Chapter I

INTRODUCTION

THERE are many people at the present day who from time to time become aware of a curious feeling that they are excitingly and tantalizingly near to a door opening into a new place, into a hidden garden of which the keyhole is within a few inches of their groping fingers. To some of these this feeling of being on the verge comes suddenly out of the blue, as a kind of incredible possibility suggested by some chance word or some phrase in a book. Others have been haunted by it all their lives, at times faintly, at times so urgently and with such a pressing need for ascertainment that they have again and again embarked on adventures of discovery, have unlocked a door and entered a garden of dreams, only to find that it is a garden of illusion—a gaily decorated stage scene, with paper flowers and cardboard trees and an impenetrable curtain behind. Falling in love is frequently an adventure of this kind, and yet the man who has had that experience, who has walked through the garden and come up against the painted drop-scene at the back, very often feels not that he is a fool but that he is being befooled; that the flowers *were* real, that the drop-scene is a stupid practical joke, and that love may really lead into a beyond, and not necessarily into a cul-de-sac. The passionate experience which shattered his everyday automatisms and altered all his values was the reality, his humdrum and somnolent daily level of half-awareness and boredom is the sham. Nevertheless, he somehow loses the reality and must needs put up with the sham. Such experiences recur, indeed they are as common as motor accidents; and they tend to convince the seeker that his intuition of a deeper and wider reality, of a crack in the wall of the every-day, is not a delusion—is not, to use the psychological jargon of the day, a wish-fulfilment fantasy.

I was talking once to some children about the credibility or incredibility of a certain supernormal experience, as happening at the present day and not in a remote biblical era. Their almost unanimous opinion was that such things could not be, 'because if they were everyone would know about them—they'd be in the paper'. 'Quite so,' said I, 'and if you yourself had a tremendous spiritual experience would you put it in the paper?' To which the equally unanimous answer was, 'No, rather not; you'd simply hate to.' From the days of

Hamlet and Horatio, and probably from the days of Noah, there have been the few who have actually heard the voice of God, and the many who have repudiated the possibility 'because if it were true it would be in the newspapers and everyone would know about it'.

Besides the abortive experience of falling in love —for however satisfying this may be emotionally it very rarely fulfils its promise of an abiding spiritual contentment—there is another blind alley down which the spiritually adventurous person of whom I am talking is likely to go, namely that of illusory religious experience.

There have always been some people in the world for whom religion, the orthodox religion of the day, is the means of opening a new door of consciousness; but for many, on the contrary, it acts as a barrier. In childhood and youth one is taught that in religion, if anywhere, lies reality. The child, still immersed in the delusion that his elders are all-wise, looks dutifully in the direction in which they point, and accepts the religious training which they offer or provide, expecting in due course to behold a great light. As time goes on and no light appears he feels that he must be spiritually blind, and, unable to admit to his elders a disease so shameful, he must needs pretend to see. In most orthodox religions there is some ceremony of initiation by which children are admitted into communion with the Church, and in the course of which they are expected to undergo a spiritual awakening or regeneration. As a rule the ceremony is led up to by a fairly elaborate preparation in which the priest or teacher instructs the candidates and impresses upon them the magnitude and crucial spiritual import of that which is about to befall them. Keyed up to expect a sensible miracle, and in fact aware of nothing but a little mild and pleasurable excitement, it is at this juncture in life that they very commonly lose once and for all their sense of spiritual values. For as a result of confirmation or the corresponding ceremony of their religion,[1] they are faced with two alternatives. Either the whole thing is a sham, a conventional figment of the grown-up world, like the ceremony of top-hats or the ceremony of paying calls; or else, and this is a much more deadly alternative, the faint glimmer of pious excitement that they felt when they were confirmed *is* the Celestial Fire, and all the lovely and burning phrases of religious language were never meant to be taken literally. In that case the painted dropscene is as far as one can ever expect to penetrate and it is only a fairy-tale that there is anything beyond. Still, a tallow dip is better than black dark-

[1] The author does not wish to call in question the spiritual validity of confirmation, but merely to draw attention to certain psychological phenomena frequently found in connexion with it.

ness, and one had better pretend to be satisfied and make the best of it. Obviously very few children follow out consciously a consecutive train of thought such as is here indicated, but this is what passes in a more or less dim way through many minds.

This type of experience is so common that almost everyone who reads these pages will have been through it in one form or another, not merely once in adolescence but possibly many times as life goes on. From it a considerable number of people emerge who in spite of repeated disillusionment are still convinced that the pearl of great price does actually exist, and that if they could but find it it would prove indeed a pearl, and not an iridescent synthetic globule.

It is to such people as these that this book is primarily addressed with the object of considering some of their problems. What is it in us that for ever insists on the worthwhileness of spiritual adventure? Why do such adventures again and again end in frustration? Is it possible to come to any definite and satisfying understanding with this craving for interior happiness, or is the level at which we habitually live the best that we have a right to expect?

That we should have to ask ourselves such questions as these argues an abysmal ignorance of ourselves and of our entire psychic mechanism, and one of the reasons why there is at present this wave of desire for more real spiritual experience is that modern psychology has begun to make us conscious of our self-ignorance. Analytical therapy has given to a great many people a touchstone, a means of distinguishing between reality and fantasy, and has incidentally destroyed for them many of their most comfortable and anaesthetizing delusions. Awakened from a state of numb neutrality to an awareness of acute dissatisfaction, they are driven to hunt for something more satisfying. Hence the crucial questions of analytical therapy, what it can accomplish and what are its limitations, are relevant to the matter in hand.

In the thirty or forty years since the beginning of modern analytical therapy—I say 'modern' advisedly, since it seems to me probable that the idea of psychotherapy is as old as civilization—there have been two main sections of opinion about it. The dramatic miracles of healing which it wrought in cases of shell-shock during and just after the War led those who came into direct contact with it to regard it as the greatest medical and educational discovery of the age, a veritable panacea for the ills of body and mind incidental to modern life. Another large body of opinion took the extreme opposite view, and considered psychotherapy to be a very dangerous and questionable method, productive of little good and much harm. With the passage of time both sides have modified their ideas. The solid worth of analytical therapy as a means of dealing with a wide and ever-widening range of maladies, physical as well as mental in their symptoms, is today pretty well established. But there were some who expected even greater things than this, and their expectations have been as yet only partially fulfilled. The degree of self-knowledge and of poise derivable from analytical treatment is such as to enable many people who have gone through it to lead as it were a new life. To themselves and to their friends they appear to have undergone a real regeneration. But a regeneration, a 're-birth', ought to be the precursor of a continuous phase of development, and it is only in rare cases that analysis leads to this. For the most part a successful analysis enables the persons to adapt to present circumstances and environment, and to meet fresh vicissitudes with greater poise and confidence than heretofore; and this very remarkable result is, not unnaturally, satisfactory and gratifying both to analyst and analysand. It is indeed no small thing to achieve a noticeable advancement in capacity for adaptation to the exigencies of everyday life. But to many the experience of analysis, seemingly at first the most real and promising spiritual adventure as yet encountered, proves in the end to be another blind alley, a means of getting thus far and no farther.

The desire to carry farther the process begun by analytical therapy has in the last decade or so occupied the minds of a number of individual analysts, though as yet tentatively rather than in connexion with organized research. A few have looked with interest in the direction of eastern psychology and philosophy and have found there suggestive and illuminating ideas, but as yet very little has been made public of the results of these researches; largely, I think, because the public is so unfamiliar with the basic elementary conceptions involved in eastern philosophy. The sources of information for English readers are books such as those of Arthur Avalon[1] or Richard Wilhelm, works of so scholarly and abstruse a nature that only the few and more serious students have the pertinacity to dig out the gems contained therein. Moreover, there are as many variants of eastern as there are of European philosophy, and to get a real grasp of even the most important of them at first hand means either a knowledge of eastern language, or the assistance of eastern scholars of no mean order to act as interpreters. As so often happens when two vast subjects of learning need to be correlated, the work is left undone because each subject is in itself the study of a lifetime, and no one person feels he has sufficient grasp of the two to venture on a comparison.

[1] Sir John Woodroffe wrote his early books under this name.

One way out of such an impasse is for some individual possessing a partial knowledge of both subjects to have the boldness to make a humble beginning. The object of this book is to undertake such a beginning by attempting a comparison between analytical psychology and yoga; yoga being one branch or aspect of eastern psychology.

But yoga again is in itself a very wide and intricate study. There are six recognized systems of Indian philosophy, ranging from the atheistic and purely materialistic, in which matter is the sole reality, to the opposite view in which matter is regarded as the shadow of spirit,[1] with no real nature of its own. Between these two extremes there is quite as much discussion on the relation between mind and matter among eastern philosophers as among those of the west. The particular system known as the *Sankhya* holds a midway position as regards this problem, a position comparable to that of the western parallelists or interactionists. It is this philosophy which more than any of the other eastern systems has been applied to practical problems of individual psychology, and which can be fruitfully used as the basis for individual experiment. In the east *experimental* psychology has gone as far as if not much farther than with us. Thousands of students

---

[1] *Spirit* and *mind* are not in the least synonymous terms in eastern philosophy, though often used as such in the west.

have experimented, and the claim is that the system of yoga training built on the sankhyan philosophy has an experimental basis in exactly the same sense as have the ordinary facts of science. If the student does so-and-so, such-and-such things will happen. If they do not happen the student has failed to comply with the directions given.

Owing to the intricacies of the subject of yoga,[1] and its general unfamiliarity in the west, I shall endeavour to make myself intelligible by confining this discussion to one widely known classic text on the subject, namely the Yoga Sutras of Patanjali. This treatise, which is based on the sankhyan philosophy, is short comprehensive and practical, is generally recognized in its native land of India as being one of the most authoritative expositions of the science of yoga, and has moreover been translated and paraphrased in several different English versions. What I hope to show by the comparison of yoga with analytical therapy is that these two have much in common, and that although yoga is perhaps an essentially eastern method, it nevertheless

[1] There are seven schools of yoga, differing from one another widely, and yet having a common aim. The system expounded by Patanjali is that of Raja (kingly) Yoga, and it includes much of the teaching of the other six. Mantra Yoga is the system of the ritualist, and emphasizes the way of union through beauty; Bhakti Yoga is the way of the devotee, very similar to that of the Christian mystic. Hatha Yoga, the best known in the west because of the spectacular asceticism of its followers, is largely concerned with bodily austerities and breathing exercises calculated to stimulate the spiritual faculties.

contains the clue needed by the west if the analytical method and theory is to reach its fullest scope as a regenerating and re-creating factor in modern life. The more thoughtful among mankind are gradually outgrowing the belief that they as individuals, or that human beings in general, are going to be 'saved' by some external intervention, and the idea is gaining ground that salvation is essentially from within.

By salvation one may take it that we mean a security of genuine happiness, for it is happiness, in the sense of poise determined by one's own inner life, that all the world is seeking. The consciously unhappy and the spiritually numb are preoccupied in filling the passing hour to the point of forgetfulness; but underneath the jazz may be recognized a growing dissatisfaction, and a deep persistent intuition that there really is a better answer to the riddle of life, not far off in a problematical heaven, but here and now. It is a Christian tradition that self-knowledge is the first step toward the kingdom of heaven. It may be that the new psychological self-knowledge of the west, strengthened by the old psychological self-knowledge of the east, will eventually give to some people an experimental proof of the reality of the world beyond the drop-curtain.

Chapter II

ANALYTICAL THERAPY—THE PRESENT POSITION

FOR about a quarter of a century the theory of analytical psychology has been before the public, and of late years analytical therapy has been increasingly recognized as a valid form of treatment. The outburst of popular excitement and opposition that accompanied its earlier phases has died down. It is no longer a newspaper topic. In fact, one may say that the time has now come when it is possible to attempt a brief survey, a review of the position. What has psychotherapy achieved? Where has it failed? Towards what is it moving?

Possibly future ages will find its greatest achievement in the fact that it has spread far and wide a new conception of the origin of disease. Many years before Freud was heard of, Christian Science and New Thought had made familiar the idea that bodily disease could be cured by purely mental treatment; but the world at large regarded these systems of thought as belonging to the realm of ethics or religion rather than of science. Psychotherapy introduced into the scientific and medical world the idea that many diseases hitherto looked upon as purely physical had a psychic origin and could be cured by a process of mental and spiritual adjustment. In the early days of analytical treatment the cases dealt with were mainly nervous and hysterical. Freud himself started in practice as a specialist in nervous diseases, and it was his deep dissatisfaction with all known treatments for this type of disorder that led him to the experiments which ultimately made his name famous.

The Great War, with its numerous cases of shell-shock, widened and clarified medical ideas concerning hysterical affections, and in a short time it came to be recognized that the old hard-and-fast distinction between an 'hysterical' and a 'real' symptom was no longer valid. It was realized that many hysterical symptoms were deep-seated and serious in their origin and not merely due to feminine or effeminate lack of self-control, while a large number of the 'real' ailments of mankind, such as indigestion, constipation, certain affections of the heart and kidneys, were frequently found to yield to psychological treatment. In recent years a number of skin diseases, such for example as chronic eczema and acne, have been added to the list of complaints which may always be at least suspected of having a psychic origin.[1] Year by year the field widens, and we are probably not far from the time

---

[1] See *Health, Disease and Integration*, by H. P. Newsholme, pub. Allen & Unwin.

when 90 per cent. or so of our physical ills will be generally recognized as having a mental and emotional cause.

To illustrate this striking change of outlook one may instance the work of the famous German analyst Groddeck. Some years ago, at a meeting of the British Psychological Society, Dr. Groddeck delivered a lecture on his theory that all of us have the ailments that suit the convenience and forward the projects of the unconscious mind, this theory applying not merely to the conventional headache, but also to the major diseases of the human race. This exposition was listened to respectfully by an audience of orthodox medical men. Nowadays, Groddeck's books on the same subject are taken seriously and accepted by many students as valid and useful.[1]

The old saw *mens sana in corpore sano* is already taking on a new meaning. More and more are we learning to expect the healthy mind to bring into being the healthy body, instead of vice versa. And this is a revolution the significance of which to the whole human race we cannot as yet begin to estimate. To take one example only, the time will come when we shall recognize that the way to free our schools from mumps, measles, chicken-pox, influenza, *et hoc genus omne*, is to alter our bad methods

---

[1] *The Book of the Id* (1927–8); *The Unknown Self* (Eng. tr. 1929).

of home and school upbringing, so that our children possess free, balanced, healthy mental and emotional consciousness. It will come to be realized that the child who catches everything is the one ill-adapted to his surroundings; he is delicate because he is unhappy, and not the reverse.

In considering the somewhat astonishing change of outlook that is taking place in regard to bodily disease as the result of the work of psychotherapists, one is apt to forget the equally important change that is slowly revolutionizing the treatment of the neurotic and the psychotic patient. Until recent years the only widely employed treatment for what is vaguely known as 'nervous breakdown' was prolonged rest, complete change of air and environment, and sedative medicines. As most people suffering from nervous collapse were unable through circumstances to take either the rest-cure or the 'complete change'—for the number of people having freedom, money and leisure is relatively small—the doctor could do very little for them save by attempting to tide things over with drugs and stimulants. Psychotherapy has provided for such cases a really hopeful and profoundly regenerative form of treatment, one that if successful is likely to prevent the recurrence of the malady, as well as curing the immediate symptoms. It is of necessity costly, but on the whole less so than six months' enforced idleness with a fair likelihood of recurrence in a few years.

As regards the insane, no form of systematic treatment save that of humane kindness and an effort at individual understanding had been widely employed until the War showed the psychiatrist the miracles that could be worked with the mentally deranged by analytical methods. At the present time, in those public hospitals for the insane where analytical treatment is systematically given to all treatable cases, it has been found that the number of cures is dramatically large.

The analyst works towards a definite goal. Just as the doctor has had as an ideal the perfectly healthy physical body, yet more often than not is obliged to rest content with the cure or amelioration of certain specific ailments, so the analyst has an established goal, the free psyche, and similarly has often to be content with some very partial degree of liberation and improvement.

This term 'free psyche' is one frequently misunderstood, for the interior personal freedom which it implies is not easily defined. Individual liberty of action must always, in the nature of things, be limited by a regard for the welfare of the community. What the analyst aims at producing is a freedom from the nervous and defensive automatisms that render men slaves of impulse and emotion, the automatism of the drunkard, the drug addict, the kleptomaniac, the chronic waverer, the choleric, the coward, the sluggard.

One of the reasons why the principles of analytical therapy are difficult for the layman to grasp is that few people are aware of the preponderance of such automatic reaction in all ordinary human conduct. This subject must be dealt with further, but for the moment it will suffice to say briefly that from the analyst's standpoint psychic freedom is largely if not entirely a matter of *awareness* in thought and action. If we were wholly self-conscious or self-aware during our waking hours we should be supermen. In that we are so little aware of our real motives and so little conscious of the implications of our daily habits we are still less than men.

Since complete psychic freedom is synonymous with human perfection, the analyst's goal will seldom be attained. When it comes to a consideration of actual achievement many analysts will probably admit to obtaining with their patients two different kinds of results, both of which might fairly be called successful. In one class the analyst is instrumental in removing the specific disabilities which have led the patient to seek his help. Such a result is often spectacular. The psychotherapist who, in relatively few treatments, can cure a condition that has appeared hopeless to the patient or even to the general medical practitioner, e.g. hysterio-epilepsy, pseudo-angina, incipient arthritis, or some deep-seated phobia which appears to verge on insanity, can justly claim to have achieved no small success, though he may only have restored his patient to the state he was in before the illness or disability occurred. Such cases were numerous in shell-shock hospitals after the War, almost indeed commonplace. There was in those days no time for further readjustment, and very often the patient neither desired nor was capable of responding to deeper treatment.

The second class is that in which the analyst finds himself able to assist the patient to inaugurate a form of mental and emotional technique which he may carry on indefinitely, with effects on character so far-reaching as to be almost incalculable. The methods employed bear a striking resemblance to those used in the preliminary stages of eastern yoga, and the results obtained are comparable; for the analysand, like the yogi, undergoes a profound and lasting alteration in character and outlook on life which is apparent not only to himself but to those in his environment.

It is perhaps useful here to glance at some of the reasons why psychotherapy has so many decriers, not only among people who speak in complete ignorance of the method but also among those who

claim to have undergone this form of treatment.

It not infrequently happens that a person undergoing analysis expects the impossible, expects to
have his character made over for him by a kind of
miracle. For a payment in cash he is to be changed
so that in future life will no longer be difficult for
him. With such people for one reason or another
the removal of immediate symptoms may be all the
analyst can effect, and this falls so far below their
expectations as to constitute to them a failure. In
these situations lie many of the so-called 'failures'
of psychotherapy. Again a very large number of
people who undertake analysis are unable to stay
the course, either because the treatment makes too
great demands in the way of self-adjustment, or because they lack patience courage and vision and
expect too quick results, or for various other reasons.
It is a fact that people of this type are very rarely
willing to admit that the treatment has been broken
off, but in nine cases out of ten they become rather
vociferous decriers of the method as being unfruit-
ful or harmful. And again, there are many cases of
actual failure in spite of the best efforts of analyst
and analysand, for no form of therapy is infallible,
and no physician can foresee and forestall all con-
tingencies.

Still another group which decries analytical treatment is composed of people who have suffered at the hands of unqualified practitioners. There is to-day no publicly recognized and standardized qualification for an analyst, and no law to prevent any one who chooses from practising. There is no such thing as a legally qualified analytical practitioner. As a result very many people without the slightest real knowledge of the subject, people who have not themselves been analysed but have merely done a little superficial reading, set out to give analytical treatment. I am not speaking only or even chiefly of deliberate fraudulent practice, but of the many honest and honourable qualified doctors who have dabbled a little in the subject, and then try it on their patients, their avowed point of view being that 'it can't do any harm and may do good'. Patients who have been treated by such people often consider themselves 'analysed', and have much to say on the futility and undesirability of the process.

In endeavouring to sum up in a few words what ground has already been won and pretty well consolidated by psychotherapists, something must be said as regards terminology and technique. In a relatively short period a large and elaborate technical vocabulary has been evolved, some of it useful, but much of it consisting merely of quasi-scientific jargon serving no purpose save that of mystifying the general public, after the manner of the ordinary medical prescription. The useful section represents a large mass of valuable and hard-won knowledge as regards the practical working of human consciousness. This includes an understanding of the influence of unconscious thinking and feeling in determining the everyday actions of normal life, and the extraordinary hold which infantile and adolescent experience still retains upon our adult outlook and decisions. The research which has crystallized into a working vocabulary descriptive of these facts is not always recognized by the orthodoxies of medicine, psychology or philosophy as being valid, because its base is an empirical one, and its justification is purely pragmatic. Thus, psychology argues that since mind and consciousness are one [*sic*] the term *un*conscious mind is absurd. The analyst replies, 'Perhaps; but practical experience shows that the thing exists'. The medical man says, 'Your cures are non-proven; what you imagine to be due to analysis is in reality due to a combination of other causes—suggestion, plus a tonic I administered at the right moment, plus the course of nature and the lapse of time'. 'Perhaps'; says the analyst, 'but in point of fact this kind of cure was not effected until I came along. If you could do it by other means, why was it not done?'

As regards technique, there is profound disagreement among analysts as among doctors and teachers. But a very real technique has indubitably been developed, so that it is possible, broadly speaking, to distinguish between the pseudo-analyst, the quack, and the real practitioner who knows his business; and this in spite of the facts above mentioned concerning the absence of recognized qualification. Although analysts may argue as to the correct position of the patient during treatment, the amount of intervention and explanation permissible, even the actual goal to be aimed at, there are nevertheless certain broad and yet definite principles upon which most of them are prepared to agree. These will be dealt with in a later chapter on the subject.

But with all the immense amount that has been done in the analytical field, there are astonishing and baffling gaps—large, obvious questions which the layman instinctively puts, only to find that the analyst has no real answer to give. Just as most of us had a flash of amazed incredulity when we first, perhaps in school-days, learnt that 'no one knows what electricity is', so in a lesser degree are we amazed to find that no one seems to know just why analysis is curative. Any explanations that exist are curiously partial and unsatisfying. A further investigation serves to show that this fact is not nearly as amazing as it seems, in view of the vagueness of orthodox psychology and philosophy in regard to certain fundamentals. Thus, if we set ourselves to find out what the learned section of humanity— to say nothing of the unlearned majority—really means by such terms as the mind, the emotions, consciousness, will, instinct, the ego, the soul, the spirit, we are confronted with indescribable vagueness and confusion. The ordinary man is prone to think, when such questions happen to present themselves in conversation, 'Well, of course, I don't exactly know what I do mean by the will, but any good book would tell you *what is generally thought*'. There lies the snare, the fallacy. We all suppose that there is a standard definition of these words that we use so glibly every day. 'Upon my soul, you are in very good spirits.' What is your soul? What are your spirits? 'Thomson is one of those weak-willed undecided chaps that never get anywhere.' We all know Thomson, and we all agree that he is weak-willed—but do we know in the least what his will is, or how it works?

There is, in the west, no body of generally accepted ideas on any of these subjects, and since we do not know what we mean by consciousness, the mind, the emotions, and the will, it is really small wonder that the analyst cannot explain to us exactly how his treatment affects our psychological make-up.

It is interesting to note that psychotherapy today is at an empirical and experimental stage comparable to that which science had reached in the middle of the nineteenth century, when science and religion were regarded as irreconcilable. Scientific observation had led to the discovery of a number of important new facts, but the general laws which underlay these facts were much more difficult to arrive at. As these laws were gradually discovered and formulated, the apparent gulf between science and metaphysics decreased, and at the present day the trend of science is somewhat in the direction of metaphysical speculation. Psychology, which is still in the stage of preoccupation with personal mechanisms, may seem hostile to the ethical and spiritual aspects of man's nature. But it may be that when the field is further explored this apparent divergence and hostility will disappear, and the validity of metaphysics, of philosophy, and even of religion may become clear to the psychologist.

It follows from what is stated above in regard to the empiricism of analytical treatment that an attempted analysis must at times do harm, exactly as surgical operations of an experimental nature may do untold harm to the individual until experience teaches the surgeon what to avoid. In the majority of cases a *properly conducted* unsuccessful analysis leaves the patient pretty much where it found him —somewhat better, somewhat worse—in a few cases very seriously worse, for there are kill-or-cure analyses just as there are kill-or-cure surgical operations. Pseudo-analysis, on the other hand, is likely to have the most dire effects on the physical, mental, and spiritual condition of the unfortunate victim.

To sum up what has been said, analytical therapy since its inception has inaugurated a new attitude toward the cause and treatment of bodily and mental disease, has established a definite technique and a working vocabulary, and has given to the world a practical knowledge of certain origins and methods in human conduct. On the other hand it is still at the almost entirely empirical stage of its development, and has contributed little of real value to our theoretical knowledge of the make-up of human consciousness—failing as it has done to answer any of the great fundamental questions concerning the existence and inter-relation of body, soul, and spirit.

Chapter III

WHAT CAUSES PEOPLE TO UNDERGO ANALYSIS OR TO UNDERTAKE YOGA TRAINING?

THE majority of people who apply to an analyst for help are ill—ill in body or ill at ease with life. There are, of course, in every analyst's practice certain cases of an acute and urgent nature demanding a category to themselves, but the general run of patients are suffering from functional nervous disorders of a not very striking nature, such as inhibit efficiency without endangering life, or from various anti-social habits that are distressing to themselves and to their neighbours. Among the former might be instanced hysterical affections, nervous disorders connected with sex and excretory functions (such as irregular menstruation, constipation, enuresis), chronic indigestion, certain skindiseases of an irritative nature; while as examples of psychological maladjustment one may cite kleptomania, over-timidity, fits of violent temper, inability to pass examinations or to settle to regular employment, unsatisfactory marriage relations, shyness and nervousness in business or social encounters, indolence, depression, drunkenness, hallucinatory delusions and so forth.

The usual history of cases of specific functional

disorder is that the patients have tried every kind of ordinary treatment—medicines, rest-cures, nature cures, patent remedies—and are none the better, or find merely temporary improvement. The other type of patient, whose difficulty is more of temperament than of bodily health, has frequently failed in one department of life after another, and has become discouraged to the verge of despair. In short, the person who goes to an analyst is most commonly one whom the medical profession has been unable to help toward physical fitness, or one who seems for some reason incapable of coping with his own life-problems.

Such people differ greatly in what they expect or demand from analytical therapy. Probably for the majority physical health is the goal, and by health they mean the absence of certain symptoms. They have a conviction that if they felt 'really fit' they could deal with life's problems pretty adequately. They are unable to realize that they are reversing cause and effect, and that it is their inadequacy to life's problems which causes the physical symptoms. This is an inherent factor in the situation. The analyst knows that what is needed before any lasting benefit can be gained is not merely the getting rid of such symptoms, but a fundamental readjustment, a thing fully as serious as a major operation on the body. A minor adjustment may relieve the troublesome ailment, but another will almost inevitably take its place before long. It should perhaps again be emphasized that I am here dealing with the ordinary 'chronic' and not with the urgent type of ill-health. Conditions of chronic physical or mental maladjustment are less generally recognized and understood than the more spectacular ones where the symptoms are dramatic and alarming and the cure rapid and apparently miraculous. Such, for example, is a well-known instance of what is technically called conversion hysteria, where a young domestic servant was disabled through a mysterious contraction of the muscles of her right hand which made the limb useless and defied all treatment. After this had persisted for months it was cured almost instantaneously by an analyst, who was able to bring to the girl's conscious realization the fact that her useless hand was a protest against earning her own living when her deep unconscious desire was to go home and take care of her sick father. When she faced the actual situation the muscles relaxed at once, and a little massage completed the cure. Nothing more was needed. Such instances are common enough but are definitely outside the scope of the present book, which deals with methods of more fundamental adjustment in physical and psychological disorders of various kinds.

Although it is probable that the majority who consult an analyst aim at re-establishing physical health, there are those who feel from the first that health is for them a by-product and not their primary objective. These people realize up to a point that their difficulties are psychological. Sometimes, as has been said, they complain that they are nervous, shy, ill at ease in company or in business relations, that they 'don't seem able to make friends'; or again they have static moral conflicts which go on for years unresolved. There are men who cannot reconcile their sexual needs with their moral standards; women who cannot find courage to throw off the unreasonable demands of selfish or bigoted parents; artists who for some hidden reason have become unproductive; deeply religious people who cannot reconcile their adult ideas of god-likeness with their childhood's teaching about God. All these are desirous primarily of coming to terms with what Freud has called the super-ego, the deep personal standard of right and wrong that is akin to conscience and yet more intimate, the sense which a man has of what he ultimately owes to himself—the thing that causes the sterile artist, no matter what his 'morals' may or may not be, to feel himself a worthless cumberer of the earth. People with this type of difficulty are satisfied if they can resolve these personal conflicts, if instead of nervousness and anxiety they can achieve ease of manner, poise, a balanced view of life, a comfortable *modus vivendi*. And these are no mean achievements. They frequently demand months or even years of searching analysis, and bring undreamed-of relief and fresh hope, not only to the patient himself but to all who are in contact with him.

And what of the student of yoga? Is there any resemblance between the position of the would-be yogi and the analysand? I think it can be said that there is much resemblance as well as a profound difference. The student of yoga is necessarily one who is dissatisfied with his own adaptation to life and to the external world; for no other reason would be sufficient to induce a man to engage in an exacting course of training which he knows from the outset will strain all his powers to the uttermost. Moreover, since such deep dissatisfaction brings conflict and tension, he is likely to be one who suffers from the nervous fatigue ill-health and ill-success in ordinary life that characterize the candidate for analysis. But there are two very important points of difference. In the first place the student of yoga *is* a student and not a patient; he approaches the question from the active and not the passive standpoint. He is prepared to work hard at his self-appointed task, to seize opportunities, to take advantage of hints, to try experiments, and above all to admit as a matter of course that the onus of success or failure lies with himself alone.

The candidate for analysis, on the other hand, goes to the analyst as to any other doctor, expecting him to take the whole responsibility of the treatment and to bring about a cure. The analyst is thus at a serious disadvantage, for whereas an ordinary physician can administer to a trusting patient drugs calculated to produce certain physical effects without the least conscious assistance from the patient himself, the analyst can do nothing at all without the co-operation of the analysand. If the mental state of a person is such that he cannot give any co-operation—as in certain though not by any means all types of insanity—then he cannot be analysed. Hence when the analysand assumes that the onus of cure is entirely on the analyst, the first and often the crucial difficulty of the case may consist in rousing him from a passive to an active attitude.

The fact that the student of yoga is aware that success depends on his own efforts is, however, not necessarily an unmixed advantage. For just as strained physical effort defeats itself by leading to rigidity (a result common in such pursuits as dancing and skating, where poise is the secret of success), so strained effort after that psychic poise and balance which is of the essence of yoga may have the effect of enhancing and reinforcing the undesirable attitude of mind against which it is directed. Among eastern students, whose psychological make-up is different from ours, this tendency to rigidity and to the forcing of a mental attitude is less prevalent than in the west; but a considerable number of Europeans who attempt yoga training, usually with little or no guidance, fail to make any progress through the increased rigidity that their very efforts induce.

The eastern student of yoga, who almost invariably works under the guidance of a teacher, is taught by specific exercises to attain relaxation of body and of mind as a condition preliminary to any advanced training. The analyst, who often repudiates entirely the attitude of a teacher,[1] nevertheless is obliged to begin his work by explaining to his patient the principle of free association, i.e. the necessity for letting the mind and emotions express themselves without restraint during treatment; and this is, in effect, a method of mento-emotional relaxation. It is not a usual analytical practice to teach bodily relaxation as such, but the analyst is accustomed to observe closely any signs of physical tension in his patient, and he has his own technique for dealing with these and for eliminating them.

[1] Schools of psychotherapy differ considerably on this point.

The need for relaxation in analysis as in yoga arises from the fact that in both methods the first step consists in the letting go of old automatisms of thought and feeling. It is the nature of the human mechanism to set or harden into fixities of habit, and this is true not only of the body but of the mind and the emotions. Speaking figuratively, it is as though the mento-emotional nature tended to harden like the stuff in an old glue-pot. The material must be brought to a perfectly homogeneous fluid consistency, and the relaxation of habitual restraint is comparable to a melting process. In the process of melting hard lumps collect on the surface, and are either dissolved by additional heat or skimmed off and thrown away. In analysis the equivalent of this is achieved by the persistent effort of the psychotherapist to produce an uncensored flow of free association in the analysand, who is required to express any ideas or images that float into his mind, regardless of rationality consecutiveness and conventional propriety. In course of time this practice brings to the surface of consciousness a great deal of unwholesome and unsound material, old hardened ideas and feelings that need to be examined, and either brought into harmony with actual known facts or else discarded. For example, no sane adult would deliberately aver that God is an old man with a white beard who is easily annoyed, and yet

many a person has never really disintegrated in his
consciousness this childish picture. Ideas of such a
kind when they float to the surface in analysis are
naturally at once discarded. They are lumps to be
fished out of the pot. Again, many a grown-up
person feels it utterly impossible to put into words
such a fact as that when he was an infant of five he
bit his little brother and lied to his nurse. The incident has coagulated in his mind as the unspeakable crime which in babyhood it was made by his
elders to appear. It still has the five-year-old emotional value which was stamped on it at a time
when sense of proportion and capacity to judge
were embryonic, and it forms part of the adult's
emotional concept of himself, part of his irrational
sense of inferiority. Brought to the surface, it needs
melting into homogeneous consistency with the
adult point of view. What do you really think now
of a baby who bites and lies? Is he an unspeakable
criminal, or merely an untrained little animal? In
this way the analyst helps the patient to relax a
great deal of emotional tension that has been unconscious, and yet definitely wasteful of nervous
energy.

Patanjali considers that this clearing and cleans-
ing of the mento-emotional nature is accomplished
by certain preliminary exercises which he sets forth
in his book, a process which will be dealt with later

in some detail. The idea here put forward is that both the candidate for analysis and the candidate for yoga enter upon their undertaking because they are, more or less self-consciously, dissatisfied with their own adaptation to life; and that for both there is prescribed a preliminary training in deep mental and emotional relaxation, with the object of loosening rigidities of thought and feeling which education and environment have set up.

Chapter IV

THE SENSE OF INSECURITY AND THE SEARCH FOR GOD

DEEP dissatisfaction with life as it appears to be and with the individual's personal adaptation to the conditions of everyday experience are universal among mankind, and are not the symptom of any one age or race or stage of civilization. In every age, moreover, there are a few people who are acutely conscious of this dissatisfaction, and whose lives are spent in a prolonged endeavour to find the remedy for it and to help their fellow men to make use of this remedy when found. These pioneers have been for the most part founders of religions and of philosophies, and their search has usually been a feeling out for some experience of or contact with a something that they called God. They have maintained that in the experience of union with God lies the only assuagement of human unrest.

In the preceding chapter it has been indicated that people who undergo analysis or become candidates for yoga belong also to the ranks of the dissatisfied, and yet their search is not avowedly a search for God, but rather a striving after self-knowledge and self-realization.

Two interesting questions arise from this situation. In the first place one asks, is the dissatisfaction which leads people to the pursuit of analysis or of yoga a thing fundamental to humanity and essentially the same as that which urges to supreme effort the mystic and the evangelist, or does the unrest of the latter spring from a specifically religious craving and that of the former from quite another source?

Again, is the achievement of the analysed person or that of the yogi related to and comparable with the achievement of the religious devotee and the mystic? Or are we to regard the attainment of self-understanding self-awareness and self-direction without any conscious religious motive as a step towards some quite different goal?

As a method of approach to these questions it is useful to consider what the idea of God stands for to the ordinary person. What does such a person think and feel about God, and what does he expect from God?

Primitive man thinks of his gods as being powerful, yet not all-powerful, easily offended and hence to be feared and propitiated; and he expects of them, if duly propitiated, food and shelter, reasonably good weather, protection from pestilence, plenty of male children, and success in battle. This is true not only of the savage but also of the simpleminded section of civilized communities, and what it amounts to is that when man feels himself to be at the mercy of forces which he does not understand and cannot control he looks to some power greater than his own for protection against the all-pervading insecurity of existence.

In proportion as he learns to control or to protect himself against the forces of nature the human being ceases to appeal for divine aid in regard to them, but no amount of material prosperity will permanently overcome his sense of insecurity. It merely happens that as he ceases to feel anxiety about the primary necessities of existence he has more time to feel the subtler and less immediate but no less poignant uncertainties of life, and these replace the former needs in his appeals for help from God.

A study of popular religious phraseology, and more especially of well-known hymns, demonstrates this point very clearly; for popular hymns are usually spontaneous emotional outbursts unfettered by dogma. To quote almost at random:

> Abide with me; fast falls the eventide:
> *The darkness deepens*; Lord, with me abide.

> *Change and decay* in all around I see;
> O Thou *who changest not*, abide with me.

> From endless ages thou art God,
> *To endless years the same.*

> Be Thou our guard while troubles last,
> And our *eternal home.*

Hide me . . . till the *storm of life be past.*

Lead, kindly Light, *amid the encircling gloom.*

Keep Thou my feet; I do not ask to see—

The recurring thought is that of human life as dark, and full of change and menace. In God is changelessness, protection, guidance, and everlasting security.

Most of the fears and uncertainties by which human beings are beset can be grouped under one of two headings—fear of change, and fear of doing wrong.[1] Fear of change may be said to include fear of discomfort and privation, of disease, of death; of loss of friends, social status, enjoyment; and, generally speaking, fear of what the next day will bring. Fear of doing wrong is closely connected with self-esteem, and is an unwillingness to fall short of accepted standards, a dread of ridicule, of making a wrong choice, of incurring the wrath of God or man, and of being punished therefor.

To calm and assuage these fears we have from infancy instinctively looked for an external source of aid, and from this external source we have expected protection that we may be guarded against all the instabilities of life, and guidance to prevent us from making mistakes.

---

[1] For those readers who are interested in the Freudian point of view one might note that fear of doing wrong touches the super-ego, and that fear of change is an id-reaction.

There is one period in our lives and one only when this craving for external protection and guidance can be fully satisfied. In normal and happy childhood it is right and natural that all needs should be supplied by parents, those omnipotent and omniscient beings who advise us correctly, absolutely correctly, in all our difficulties, and who have absolute power to protect us from all dangers. These god-like beings are never wrong, never afraid, never at a loss. They exist in order to answer our prayers, to punish us when we do wrong and to reward us when we do right. They have many privileges that are denied to us, and they are often angry, revengeful, irritable and ill-tempered; but we do not consciously consider these things wrong in them, though we know they would be wrong in us. This last is a very significant point, and one that is often overlooked. The child's earliest conception of the absolute, and hence of God, is of a being who has a right to do what is wrong for himself. This is probably one reason why he does not seriously question the Old Testament idea of an angry, jealous, revengeful and blood-thirsty Jehovah. He accepts the dictum 'Vengeance is mine; I will repay, saith the Lord', as being natural enough, because it is precisely the parental attitude.

As we grow out of babyhood we gradually lose these divine beings—our absolute becomes a relative. It may be that one day we see our mother badly frightened. She is not omnipotent after all. Our father punishes us with manifest injustice. He is not infallible. Bit by bit we learn that grown-up people are not the mighty giants we thought them, but relatively feeble creatures like ourselves, and we are obliged to look elsewhere for guidance and security.

At this stage, when individual character begins to develop, there is a natural divergence according to type. The desire for security is universal, and the realization that parents cannot satisfy it is inevitable; but a relatively small number of people deliberately face these facts and try to discover a solution. The majority are content to find some means of evading and forgetting the issue. While realizing perforce that parents are fallible, they nevertheless cling to the parental fantasy by a kind of deliberate convention, inimitably phrased by A. P. Herbert:

> As my poor father used to say
>   In 1863;
> And what my father used to say
>   Is good enough for me.

For the rest, they contrive to be 'too busy to think about morbid things like that'.

Of the section who prefer to treat life more directly and seriously it is perhaps true to say that the majority pass through a phase of accepting or trying to accept the conventional orthodoxy of their environment. For these adolescence is a period of confusion and bewilderment, during which the problems and inconsistencies of orthodox religion inexpertly presented by parents and teachers are a source of conflict and doubt, sometimes repressed for years, but sooner or later becoming clamorous.

This period of confusion varies greatly in duration, but very commonly lasts far beyond physical adolescence and into the late twenties or early thirties. In some cases it is a prolonged state of repression, characterized by repeated effort to adapt the rising tide of life within oneself to the exterior standard for which circumstances or environment have presented a strong argument. Such standards may be religious in the ordinary sense of the word, or they may be social cults derived from family tradition. In other cases the period is one of trial and error, during which solution after solution is accepted, tried, and found inadequate.

At this point it often happens that an enthusiasm for a cause or for a new idea takes hold of the individual and absorbs him to the exclusion of all else. In that it is absorbing it tends to assuage unrest and dissatisfaction with life, and in that it is self-chosen and new it seems to offer a better chance of security than the inherited orthodoxy which has been found wanting. Usually these causes or movements which absorb so many of the choice spirits of the day are progressive, altruistic, and social in their aims, and therefore provide an excellent form of what the analyst calls sublimation, that is, the transmutation of personal conflict into useful activity. These are, nevertheless, in the nature of solutions from without, and the man who becomes possessed by a cause or a movement, as so many do, tends to crystallize, or, to use another figure, ceases to travel in a spiral and begins to gyrate in a circle.

The true adventurer in the world of the spirit, the man who has the courage to insist that there is something behind the painted drop-scene, has to learn the invalidity of every form of exterior support, to achieve security by finding a centre of gravity within himself. When this is found he may work for whatever cause he chooses, but he still continues to travel in a forward direction, because he is free in spirit and not obsessed by anyone idea.

This search within as contrasted with the search without marks the basic distinction between two methods of attempting to deal with man's sense of insecurity, and both are as old as philosophy itself. In the New Testament it lies at the root of the famous controversy between 'faith' and 'works'; in the science of religion there are the two aspects of divinity, God Immanent and God Transcendent; in all religious reformations the fundamental conflict is between the point of view of those who lay stress on ceremonial and organized religion, and of those who hold that interior experience alone is valid. In its earlier stages Luther's revolt was against the formalism, the *mechanism* of the Catholic Church. John Wesley's great appeal was not concerned with new doctrine, but with the need for intimate personal experience. The teaching of Christ was not aimed at destroying the Jewish religion, but at breaking up its rigid and petrifying formalities in order that its spiritual possibilities might be freed and expanded. Religious revival is, in fact, always due to an uprush of living experience breaking through encrusted forms.[1] As has been said, the human mind tends to set in moulds which then lose their vitality and need from time to time to be broken. Forms are necessary, but need to be held responsive to the changes of life.

For our present purpose it is sufficient to point out that the religious mystic, the candidate for analysis, and the student of yoga all belong to the group of those who seek the interior solution, although each of the three has a different method of approach and a different working hypothesis.

The mystic (not necessarily the Christian, since mysticism is common to all great religions) pre-

[1] Cf. the speech of the Pope in Browning's *Ring and the Book* (Bk. X, ll. 1864 et seq.).

supposes the existence of a deity, an immanent or interior God, and his entire energies are devoted to achieving conscious union with or experience of that divine being.

The person who undertakes analysis presupposes nothing in the nature of a dogma or belief, his sole hypothesis being that self-knowledge is worth attainment. He seeks valid inner experience, of whatever nature it may prove to be. Hence the mystic is in the position of an explorer looking for something he knows to exist—such as the North Pole, or the source of a river; while the analysand is, as it were, merely exploring an unknown country with no preconceived notions of its physical features. Both these methods of approach have their advantages and their drawbacks. A definite preconceived goal makes for speed and enthusiasm, but also tends to self-deception. To set out on a voyage of discovery without any definite goal makes an unbiased explorer; but the weak point of analytical therapy at its present stage is precisely its lack of a clear objective. The journey is apt to come to an inconclusive end because the traveller gets tired and thinks he has gone far enough.

The method of approach in yoga is again quite different, though approximating both to the analytical and to the mystical. In yoga as in the mystic experience there is a definite goal, which the yogi calls kaivalya or liberation. As in analysis there is always an analyst, so in yoga there is always a teacher—but the teacher of yoga has a far more definite idea of what constitutes the attainment of kaivalya than has the average analyst of what constitutes an adequate analysis. This is not surprising when one considers that the systems of yoga are the result of two thousand years or more of research and experiment, while analytical therapy in modern form is not yet fifty years old.

Yoga takes a position in regard to the existence of God that is utterly unfamiliar to the European. Patanjali says that if the student is of such a temperament that the idea of God appeals to him, this is to be encouraged, for the approach to liberation through devotion to God is rapid. If, on the other hand, the student is unable to accept the hypothesis of God, then there are other equally sure paths of approach. This idea is so foreign to western minds that it will be necessary to discuss it later in detail (see Ch. VI). It will suffice here to say that it involves no belittlement of the conception of God and no insincerity of approach to him; but is based rather on the hypothesis that the undisciplined human mind is incapable of grasping or even conceiving the things of the spirit. The candidate for yoga is recognized as blind to the spiritual life, inexperienced in and ignorant of its validities, and so he cannot 'know' God. If he be of religious temperament then he is fortunate, in that he can accept the hypothesis of a Supreme Being; but if that type of faith is impossible to him, he need not therefore renounce the practice of yoga. Religion in the east is not conceived as personal emotion but partakes of the nature of science, and the scientific approach of the eastern philosopher to a subject which in the west has for so many centuries been regarded as at war with science is one of the many obstacles in the path of mutual understanding between east and west; one, too, which it is well to face at the outset of our consideration of yoga.

The goal of yoga is the attainment of liberation from human imperfections and uncertainties, and hence the practice is a definite and conscious attack upon the problem of insecurity. Its method is to train the whole nature to respond to conscious control and self-direction, and it claims that when self-awareness and the capacity for spiritual insight are achieved, perception of real values can be sustained, and this brings with it a sense of complete security. In such a state of consciousness the problem of the existence or non-existence of God can be suitably considered, the yogi now having reached a point where he is capable of apprehending spiritual realities.

To sum up, it would seem that the sense of insecurity is a basic human experience. In childhood it finds its right and normal assuagement through parental care and guidance, but in later life it becomes urgent once more, and is the cause of all spiritual adventure, and indeed of most human enterprise. The striving after rest and security is universal because it arises from the desire for continued existence, and this, says Patanjali, is ineradicable in the saint as in the sweeper.

Of the countless ways in which man has tried to satisfy the longing, some have led him by the path of activity to an exterior solution, and some by the path of contemplation to an interior peace. In the east the search has been for the most part a search within, and the Yoga Sutras of Patanjali are an epitome of what eastern experience has found out about the interior or contemplative method. In the west the search within has been the method of the few, and those few have been religious devotees. Analytical therapy is a scientific method of attaining interior equilibrium, and as such approximates to the contemplative rather than to the active tradition. In this respect it resembles yoga, and the attitudes of the two methods to the question of the existence of God, although by no means identical, have points of resemblance. Yoga as we have seen advocates but does not insist on the devotional approach. In the early days of psychotherapy the religious type of sublimation was looked on some-what dubiously, but in this respect the analytical point of view has tended to modify, and at the present day a considerable number of analysts would agree with Patanjali as to its value. The current phrase is that 'religion is one of the best types of sublimation'.

One of the outstanding merits of analytical therapy is that it provides, for the first time in the history of western exoteric thought, a method of interior approach and interior experience for the agnostic as well as for the religious type of mind. In this respect alone, had there been no other, the resemblance between it and yoga would have been sufficiently noteworthy to invite comparative study of the two methods.

Chapter V

THE DEVELOPMENT OF ANALYTICAL THEORY AND TECHNIQUE

IN the preceding chapter the question of human insecurity and the universal search for peace were briefly dealt with, and it was indicated that analytical therapy came into being through the fundamental nature of this need. The point of view of the analyst in relation to the problem was not discussed in any detail, but was assumed to follow certain lines.

We must however admit that it is as unsound to generalize freely about the analyst as about 'the child' or 'the average man'. Although the analyst's problem is always fundamentally the same, in that he has to deal with maladies that are the outcome, either directly or indirectly, of fear and a sense of insecurity, and although there are certain basic truths about the human mind and its workings which all analysts would admit as axiomatic, yet the various schools of psychotherapy differ very widely in their theories, their methods, and their idea of the legitimate scope of analytic treatment.

In order to make any fair comparison between psychotherapy and yoga some degree of familiarity with the main schools of psychotherapy is required, and perhaps the best way to achieve this is to survey briefly the history and development of the movement.

A few years ago it was approximately true to say that there were three schools of analytical therapy, originated by Freud, Adler, and Jung respectively. The situation is no longer so clear-cut, for these schools have ramified, and there are analysts of repute who do not identify themselves with any of them. For the present purpose, however, it will be sufficient to trace the development of the three, and to refer to a few of their more important offshoots.

Sigmund Freud was born in Moravia in 1856, of very poor Jewish parents. The family shortly moved to Vienna, where he worked his way to the university by scholarships, and in due course qualified as a doctor. The Viennese school of medicine, though one of the best in the world, had not as yet even begun to suspect what is a truism in medicine to-day, namely, that physical symptoms can be induced by the mind. Before actually starting in practice Freud took a year in Paris, and there met with a piece of good fortune that altered the whole course of his life and was the indirect cause of his becoming in later years world-famous. He fell in with Charcot and his even more renowned pupil Janet, two investigators who had been studying the phenomena of hypnotism, and had succeeded in demonstrating that under hypnosis all manner of physical symptoms could be induced by suggestion—burns, swellings, paralysis, anaesthesia, and so forth. They described the state produced by hypnosis as dissociation of consciousness,[1] and established the fact that in the hypnotic or dissociated state a person could have many ideas of which he was in his waking state entirely unaware. In other words, these experiments had taken the first step towards demonstrating the reality of the unconscious mind, the basic conception on which all analytical therapy depends. While Charcot and Janet used hypnosis a great deal for the cure of physical disease, it never seems to have occurred to them to utilize dissociated states of consciousness as a means of diagnosing and dispersing mental troubles.

On his return to Vienna Freud set up as a nerve specialist, but became increasingly dissatisfied with the orthodox methods of treating nervous disorders, which he considered to be merely palliative and unproductive of lasting effect. At this juncture he came into contact with an older man, also a nerve specialist, who gave him the clue to his subsequent discoveries. This man, Breuer by name, described to Freud a curious and interesting case he had recently had of a woman who suffered from paralytic symptoms, disorders of speech, and somnam-

[1] See Hart, *Psychopathology*, p. 36.

bulism. Breuer had hypnotized her and got her to talk of her symptoms under hypnosis. He found that in this condition she tended to trace back any given symptom to its origin or first occurrence, and moreover that each symptom when thus traced disappeared and did not recur. He also found, though he did not attach any great significance to the discovery, that all the hysterical symptoms led back to occasions connected with her father, to whom she was deeply attached in a childish and dependent way, and of whom she was also very much afraid.

For several years after this Breuer and Freud both used hypnosis regularly, and Breuer was so satisfied with the method that he never departed from it. With Freud this was not the case. He soon found that cures by hypnosis were uncertain and often only temporary, the reason apparently being that the patient in waking consciousness was sometimes unable to remember even with the doctor's help what had been revealed under hypnosis ; yet the cure was dependent on the full linking up of the two states of consciousness.

Freud accordingly began to experiment with other methods of touching the unconscious. Soon he found that by getting his patients into a dreamy half-state he could arrive at their difficulties, and later he succeeded in elaborating a skilled technique by which he could treat the patient while fully awake. Thus from the very outset the method of hypnosis was rejected, and it has never, in spite of a widespread idea to the contrary, formed part of genuine analytical technique.

Within the next few years Freud had developed and set forth the theories which have since made him famous, and had gathered round him in Vienna a group of devoted adherents to whom his slightest word was law. This group met weekly at his house, discussed, listened, and compared notes, and regarded their privilege of membership in the Wednesday night assembly as a thing of priceless worth, which indeed it was. Such in brief is the history of the first beginnings of analytical therapy.

In his early years Freud was of necessity an empiricist, and by temperament a pragmatist. His work was wholly experimental, and his experiments were essentially different from those of the laboratory. He was working on human beings, and his primary concern was not to demonstrate a theory but to bring about a cure. He had no chance of being able, as the ordinary scientist is able, to prove his hypotheses by a great number of experiments of an exactly similar nature from which all disturbing factors were carefully eliminated. He and his immediate followers were obliged to accept for working purposes and to disseminate as fact much that was not really established, and that is still after thirty or forty years regarded as controversial.

The early and still valid generalizations set forth by Freud have always been known as the Freudian mechanisms, and this term mechanism is in itself indicative of the practical rather than philosophical or strictly scientific nature of the work done at this time by Freud and his followers. They were interested in the working of the mind, not in its origins, and were too busy in these early days to heed the theoretical objections to their ideas raised by orthodox psychologists. The most famous and basic of the mechanisms were those termed the unconscious mind, the libido, repression, the oedipus complex, and the transference; and from these the elaborate later technique with its even more elaborate terminology has been gradually built up.

Following up and developing the theories of Charcot and Janet, Freud postulated three 'areas' or states of mind, the unconscious, the pre-conscious, and the conscious.

The unconscious mind, the basic conception in analytical therapy, has been so much written about that it is not easy to find a simple and yet generally admitted definition of it. For our present purpose it may suffice to describe it as the receptacle of our entire past experience from birth. Some authorities incline to accept the idea that it includes pre-natal experience, and some that it includes racial past experience as well.

The pre-conscious is the threshold between the conscious and the unconscious. It contains material that is not at the moment in consciousness but can be recalled at will. Thus, I do not at the moment know what I was doing last Tuesday afternoon, but with an effort I could probably remember, since this fact is in my pre-conscious.

A common misapprehension in regard to the unconscious is to suppose that it also can be tapped by a direct effort of the will. Much of the content of the unconscious moves quite freely through the pre-conscious stage into consciousness, but certain parts of our past experience are definitely repressed. These parts are not amenable to conscious effort nor reachable by any ordinary introspection, and this is why self-analysis is almost impossible. Freud's discovery of the delicate and intricate technique by which such repressed material can be reached was his great achievement. It is of course possible to learn the art of applying this technique to one's self, but even expert analysts are sometimes baffled in their attempts to elucidate their own problems and have to seek the aid of a colleague.

Freud's theory was that in our ordinary waking life ideas and impulses originate in the unconscious, where they are experienced as emotion but not thought in words. They either pass freely thence across the threshold of the pre-conscious into consciousness, or else are repressed before reaching the threshold and remain unconscious.[1] It is in the pre-conscious stage that they take on verbal form. Those ideas are repressed which if they became realized and conscious would cause such disagreeable emotions as of shame, fear, disappointment.

Freud was a good deal puzzled to define the process by which *unconscious* ideas are repressed, for it must be realized that repression, in the technical sense, is not a conscious process. To explain repression he postulated a mechanism which he called the endopsychic censor, having the power of shutting the door between the conscious and the unconscious. At first he made no attempt to explain the term censor, and his later efforts to do so led him into paths of great interest but too intricate to be followed here.

In order to distinguish between the voluntary deletion of ideas from the mind, which is a conscious everyday mental process, and this unconscious censoring, he called the former *suppression* and the latter *repression*.

The ideas repressed into the unconscious were considered to have their own quota of energy or

[1] It should be clearly understood that whereas all repressed matter is unconscious, the whole unconscious is not repressed. See *The Ego and the Id*, by Sigmund Freud, p. 17.

life-force, and this energy, dammed up and finding no natural outlet, expressed itself in the form of neurotic or hysterical symptoms, such as phobias, tics and so forth. Freud postulated a general basic energy to which he gave the name of *libido*, and his early experiments led him to the conclusion that it was purely sexual in origin. Later on, perhaps somewhat influenced by the storm of opposition that this hypothesis aroused, he allowed his definition to widen, and was prepared to accept the idea that all forms of liking and loving, all enthusiasms and so forth, were manifestations of libido. The broadening of his original conception was acclaimed with relief by all who were interested in his theories, for the majority of students and psychiatrists found it impossible to consider sex, as such, the sole determining factor in life. In more recent years Freud and his followers have reverted once more to their original view of libido, and as a result the other schools of psychotherapy have diverged more and more from his.

Of all Freud's doctrines there was none that aroused such a vehement and angry outcry as that which postulated the sex life of the infant. As is now generally known, he maintained as a fundamental tenet that during the first three years or so of its life the child was, in a sense, largely preoccupied with sex; that the infant's interest in its own body was a manifestation of sex, and that every baby passed through an instinctual phase when it desired acutely though unconsciously to possess the parent of the opposite sex and hence to delete the parent of its own sex. This phase, being as purely instinctual as the sucking phase, was, under psychologically healthy environmental conditions, outgrown in the natural process of development. But when during the first years this natural instinct had been unduly thwarted, where through the advent of another baby or for some similar cause the child did not receive what he considered to be his fair share of parental attention, then the infantile phase tended to persist and to become a source of neurosis. This mechanism was named the oedipus complex, from the old Greek story of King Oedipus, who being in the legend unaware of his parentage killed his father in order that he might possess his mother.

The mechanism of the transference is another widely misunderstood Freudian concept. The popular idea at one time was that the transference consisted in the patient's falling in love with the analyst, and that his doing so indicated a fatuous lack of self-control, and was quite unnecessary. In former days the analysts themselves somewhat lent colour to this idea, for the important part of the analytical process was considered to be the bringing to light of specific 'complexes' and exploding them, the transference being a secondary matter. To-day the majority of analysts regard it as a crucial factor in the treatment of any case.

In actual fact the transference is not synonymous with the patient's 'love' for the analyst, and is quite as often expressed in terms of hatred, anger, resentment or scorn. In the course of analytical treatment a good deal of old and forgotten emotional experience comes to the surface, connected with people who have been of significance to the patient in the past—such people as parents, brothers and sisters, nurses, teachers. As these associations come up the patient finds himself unconsciously transferring to the analyst the emotions he has felt in times past for this or that person. The analyst becomes in turn the father, the sister, the lover, the nurse; and on to him is projected the patient's corresponding mood of rebellion, irritation, unsatisfied desire, jealousy, child-like dependence and the like. This is the transference, the process of transferring to the analyst unsatisfied emotion left over from some earlier experience; and present-day methods of analysis are largely concerned with analysing and making conscious the transference itself. This process in proportion as it is successful has the twofold effect of freeing the patient from the trammels of his old, largely unrealized and confused emotions, and also from his fantasied dependence upon the analyst.

At first sight it may seem that this mechanism is improbable and not in accordance with ordinary human conduct. Further consideration shows us, however, that we do more or less habitually vent emotions both pleasurable and the reverse on people and even on things that are in reality unconnected with their true cause. It is proverbial that a happy lover is in love with all the world, and similarly the man who has had cold coffee and ill-cooked bacon for breakfast vents his irritation on his blameless office staff.

These five psychological concepts of the unconscious mind, libido, repression, the oedipus complex, and the transference form the basic principles on which the subsequent elaborate psycho-analytical structure has been raised. A number of years later a further theory was elaborated and rapidly came to be regarded as fundamental, namely that of the Ego, Super-ego, and Id.

The theory itself is of such a nature and deals with such unfamiliar material that except for the experts there are few who have a clear conception of it. Reduced to its simplest terms it is approximately this: Three main factors are involved in the psychological problem of man—instinctive desires which in the Freudian terminology have been called the id, moral inhibitions constituting the super-ego, and the ego itself, which is reason based on real experience. A simple definition of this sort is bound to be misleading, for the actual theory is, as I have said, both subtle and abstruse. Freud himself defines the ego as 'a coherent organization of mental processes',[1] and by this he appears to mean that the ego is the part of us which is in contact with exterior reality, which exercises judgement and discretion, sees relationships and estimates values. It is the factor in us which determines what we call sanity, and makes us adapt our instinctual and self-interested impulses to our social environment in a constructive fashion.

The ego is developed from the id, a term first used by Groddeck and afterwards accepted, though with a not identical meaning, by Freud. Freud looks upon the mind of an individual as 'an unknown and unconscious id upon whose surface rests the ego'.[2] The development of the ego from the uncoordinated and unconscious id begins with the earliest experience of sense perception and continues throughout life. Probably one reason for the prevailing confusion in the lay mind in regard to the ego and id categories is that they introduce a cross-classification, for the ego is not synonymous with

[1] *The Ego and the Id*, p. 15.
[2] Ibid., p. 28.

the conscious mind, nor is the id the unconscious, though at first glance it seems to be so. Closer examination shows that the ego is partly conscious and partly unconscious, and so is the id. The super-ego is a special development of the rational self which Freud regards as being the direct outcome of the oedipus complex, or in other words of the relation of the child to its parents. The young child begins as he emerges from infancy to realize that he cannot exclusively possess the parent, and the process of compulsory sublimation and self-discipline which is set up when he is forced to abandon this instinctual desire results in the formation of an embryonic conscience or moral sense. In the process of recognizing himself as necessarily separate from the parent he becomes aware of the parental standards and tends to accept these as his own, usually identifying himself particularly with either father or mother. This accepting of a standard and trying to conform to it becomes a strong compulsion or a fixed mento-emotional habit, in some children an overwhelmingly strong one, and exhibits itself in the intense love of parental approbation and of approbation in general which persists until adolescence and in many cases throughout life. In later years the influence of various parental substitutes, as for example the teacher, may supersede that of the actual parent, as may the social standards of the community or group. In some circumstances and with certain temperaments the whole consciousness of the human being can become the slave of the super-ego or compulsive conformity to fixed patterns, and conduct then becomes entirely automatic and out of contact with reality. If, as has been stated, the id represents instinctual desire and the super-ego moral compulsion, it is clear that the problem of the ego, the reasonable and discriminative self, is to win his freedom from both, for if he permits either to enslave him he is lost. The problem of each individual is to maintain a balance between the self-interested instinctual nature which is his animal inheritance, and the demands of human relationships and society as a whole. This can be done only by the ego's extending further and further the field in which he is actively aware of what has hitherto been under the dominance of id and super-ego motivation. The object of analytical therapy is to produce conscious awareness of what is otherwise the deeply unconscious dominance of instinct and of compulsive moral sense.

One of Freud's early and intimate pupils was Alfred Adler. At first Adler was quite willing to accept the Freudian doctrine in its entirety, but in proportion as Freud emphasized more and more the exclusive importance of sex as the sole cause of neurosis, there came to be a widening rift between them. Adler, like Freud, was a Jew, but unlike him he was a convinced socialist, one who saw the human being always as a member of the community, and who regarded social adaptation as man's highest goal. He was a student of Nietzsche and Schopenhauer, and he held that it was not sex but the will to power which is the driving force in evolution. He maintained that every human being suffers from some sense of inferiority; it may be due to something physical, such as smallness of stature, deformity, muscular weakness, or it may be inferiority of circumstance, poverty, social ostracism, lack of education. To overcome his real or imagined inferiority he consciously or unconsciously devises some scheme of action, and this Adler calls his 'style of life'. Thus a boy who is small in stature and unable to play his part in athletics develops a sharp tongue and fluency of speech that secures him a position of importance. A woman who has had to be the family drudge, waiting on others and receiving no care herself, develops a helpless form of paralysis, and becomes an invalid whom the family are obliged to wait upon. All styles of life are not futile and harmful, for history records many noble and useful adaptations. Demosthenes the stammerer becomes a great orator; Robert Louis Stevenson, the delicate lad too frail to follow the proud family tradition of engineering, becomes a writer of prose as delicate, as skilfully put together, and as efficient for its purpose as the most elaborate of the engineer's treasured machines.

Adler is convinced that this inherent necessity to become powerful is not only the motive force that drives forward human evolution, but also the hidden cause of all neurosis. For it is the man who has hit upon an unsatisfactory 'style of life' who develops into the neurotic.

Moreover he considers that the style of life is not so much unconscious as deeply secret. The instinct of psychic preservation causes us to hug our plan to us, and to fear nothing so much as that it may be revealed and snatched from us. The more futile and useless the scheme, the more secretive is its author. The aim of analysis, according to Adler, is to discover this style or plan, and to convince the patient that he can substitute for it another which is of use to the community.

There was obviously a wide divergence of ideas between Freud and Adler, and in 1911, after a few years of close association, a definite breach occurred, and Adler and his adherents were formally asked to leave the Psycho-Analytical Society. The breach has progressively widened, and the Adlerian method is no longer called psycho-analysis, but has assumed its own title of Individual Psychology.

As Adler's connexion with Freud began to weaken, a new pupil came into prominence. A young doctor from Zurich, Carl Jung by name, had for some years been an admirer and follower of Freud, and in about 1908 began to be his close associate. Once again master and pupil worked together for a few years and then became estranged through difference of opinion. As Freud was at heart a scientist and Adler before everything else a socialist, so Jung was fundamentally a teacher and, in the wide sense of the word, a religious man. In each case the outlook on life coloured the therapeutic method. Jung came to differ from Freud as regards several vital points. Thus he believed it to be an essential part of his task as an analyst to help and teach his patients, whereas Freud declared, with more justice than seems apparent on the surface, that for the analyst to instruct and help by direct advice was an unwarrantable interference with the patient's freedom.

Again, Jung considered that Freud's idea of the libido as purely sexual did not cover the facts, and that to explain the evolution of the race from savagery to civilization some far wider hypothesis was needed. He held that libido must be defined as general psychic energy, in which sexual energy is but one factor.

He further denied the *general* validity of the

oedipus complex, and he took a different view of the unconscious, laying great stress on the fact of its containing racial memories—such memories as cause the newly hatched duckling to swim, or horses to go mad at fire, or a man to fear a treacherous something in the dark. This theory of the racial unconscious is basic in much of Jung's writing.

In due course Jung, like Adler, severed his connexion with the Freudians, and founded his own school of thought under the name of Analytical Psychology.

With the passage of time other outstanding analysts have developed theories and methods which are of great practical interest and which are tending to become embodied in the general mass of analytical theory. Groddeck with his *Book of the Id* and Ferenczi with his experiments in what he calls Active Therapy are significant, and later still Otto Rank in his *Trauma of Birth* and in subsequent writings has set forth ideas which are likely in due time to have far-reaching effects.

At the present day the position is that many analysts prefer not to identify themselves too closely with any one school, but to use whatever methods seem applicable to the case in hand ; and this approximation to the attitude which prevails in general medical practice is surely healthy and desirable. But given such variety of method it is not easy to generalize as to what analysis means and how it is carried out, since most of what it is possible to say about method and process could be queried by one or another school.

Analysis may, however, be defined as a process the object of which is to bring into consciousness those unconscious elements in the id and super-ego which are in conflict with or untrue to reality.

We are unwilling to believe, and yet it is a fact, that a comparatively small proportion of our daily feelings thoughts and actions are conscious, aware, self-chosen and self-directed. Actually many of us are content to be the prey of moods of whose real origin we are unaware. We live or endeavour to live by a system of morality that we have accepted without considering its real implications. We smoke and drink, play cards, go to dinner-parties—or, as the case may be, we go to church, sit on committees, attend conferences and belong to various organizations, not because we have chosen these activities for ourselves, but because our environment has indicated them to us, and they pass the time. We do not live our lives, but are lived, as Groddeck says, by our circumstances; by subtle, little-understood urges from within which we call 'likes' and 'dislikes', and by our passions of greed, ambition, sex, and so forth. Under some conditions and with certain temperaments the daily conflicts and the unthinkingness of life are not at all unbearable. They appear natural and inevitable, and 'what else is there?' But in times of stress and emergency values alter, latent impulses become more urgent, and the resultant conflict causes disease of mind and body. The analyst maintains that to cure such disease it is necessary to bring into consciousness and awareness its underlying and often very deep-seated origins. The fact that it is by definition impossible to reach the unconscious by a direct effort of intention obliges him to employ a skilled technique for so doing, and his chief tool is that of free association. The patient, lying or sitting in a relaxed position, is required to let his mind also relax, and to give utterance without check to every passing thought. Each idea is allowed to call up of itself the next associated picture, as in the game where one person says cat and the next must say the first word that occurs to him—dog, claws, fire, or whatever it may be. This is a difficult task, for at once the patient finds the ideas which automatically occur produce a conflict with his sense of fitness, of decency, of courtesy, of self-esteem and of humour. The very fact that he must not censor his thoughts seems to set up in him trains of association which he shrinks from exposing, and he resorts to evasions. He may find himself struck dumb, and will asseverate that he 'is not thinking of anything', or he may deliberately become alert and garrulous, and create an artificial avalanche of ideas which seem to be but are not his natural train of thought. The earlier stages of analysis are very commonly occupied by efforts on the part of analyst and analysand to establish a habit of genuine free association and free speech. In due course the patient if he is sincere in his intention learns the knack, but throughout the treatment the resistance to uncensored expression of what he is actually thinking is bound to be recurrent.

In the early days of analysis the patient's dreams were considered to be an almost essential factor, the one means whereby useful trains of free association could be started. At the present day dream-analysis plays a lesser part and is often merely incidental, though Freud laid the utmost stress on the dream as a key to the unconscious mind.

Most analysts consider the question of the transference to be a crucial one in every case treated. As has been said (p. 60) in a successfully handled analysis the patient's attitude to the analyst is always emotional, and very commonly includes love, hatred, contempt, devotion, submission, rebellion, distrust, confidence, and any other feelings that he may have experienced in his previous life for the people with whom he came in contact. It is the analyst's task to meet the varying situations between himself and his patient equably and impersonally, and by means of free association to help him to bring into consciousness the real origin of the emotions, disentangling reality from fantasy. Although some analysts make little of the transference, the more prevalent view to-day is that in the analysis of the transference lies the crux of the whole matter, and that an adequately dealt with transference is equivalent to a successful analysis. When one considers that from infancy onwards the conflicts and inhibitions of life are almost entirely concerned with social adaptation and with tangled or unfulfilled personal relationships, it seems natural enough that the transference mechanism, by which these conflicts are projected on to the analyst and resolved with his help, should be of primary importance.

The process, like that of education, is a continuous one and has no final end. As the aim of education is to fit a man to take his due place in his environment, so the aim of analysis is to enable him to meet consciously and with awareness the problems of his life, and to hold the balance between his instinctive desires and cravings and his moral, social, and spiritual compulsions and obligations. It is in so doing that he gradually conquers the sense of insecurity by finding an interior stability of soul.

Analysis has been variously received by the world at large. It has been regarded as a cheap quackery, as a diabolical enemy to religion and to purity of life, and as a new and miraculous panacea. In reality it is none of these things. That it is quackery is the cry of the completely uninformed. Cheap it is not in any sense of the word, for it requires of analyst and of patient a devotion and a sacrifice the searchingness of which is in direct ratio to the success to be hoped for. It is an enemy to automatic or sentimental religiosity and to prudery, but one of the most powerful factors in the revival or survival of the search for reality in religion and in morality. It is not a panacea, but in its deeper implications a therapy which can be successful in full measure only for the few who have spiritual courage, and a high degree of fortitude and perseverance. And finally, except in details of technique it is not new. Reduced to simplest terms the fundamental thesis of the analyst is that the ills of humanity are due to ignorance and more especially to self-ignorance, and that the way to healing is by the path of self-knowledge. But this is the teaching of the Christian fathers, and of the Buddha five hundred years before Christ, and of the Yoga Sutras of Patanjali which were, according to some authorities, written down about two hundred years before the Christian era, but were the summary of a teaching originating unknown centuries earlier still. One might safely say that probably every philosopher since the world began has arrived at the conclusion that the way to salvation lies through self-knowledge. At intervals in the world's history there are brought to birth methods by which this difficult self-knowledge may be attained, and of these it is evident that yoga is one and analytical therapy another. The two differ because they were the products of widely different races and epochs, and each was adapted to the circumstances for which it was intended. But the aims of both are similar, because the problems of humanity in all ages are similar. There is a fundamental likeness between the two systems which, at a time when we are being forced to realize the world as a unit, it is worth while to examine and to estimate.

Chapter VI

THE BASIC PRINCIPLES OF PATANJALI'S PHILOSOPHY

A GENERAL idea of the scope of this book and the nature of the material to be dealt with having now been given, I propose at this point to plunge into a somewhat detailed consideration of the philosophical and psychological ideas expressed or implied in the Yoga Sutras of Patanjali.

Practically nothing is known about the writer of the Sutras, and authorities differ widely as to his date, and even as to his identity. It is said that, himself a learned yogi, he was the disciple of a greater teacher, and that like Euclid he did not originate the system outlined in his book, but merely set down in writing certain precepts of extreme antiquity that had descended from generation to generation by word of mouth.

These rules or precepts do not set forth a philosophy, but are practical instructions for attaining certain psychological states. In writing them Patanjali assumed the fundamental tenets of his own school of philosophy, the sankhya,[1] much as

[1] See pp. 80 et seq.

a writer on the treatment of a certain disease would assume the ordinary facts of anatomy and physiology. There is little of argument or controversy in the treatise. He is telling his readers how to achieve, not what to believe.

In this country and in most western lands the idea of spiritual development by processes of meditation is inextricably bound up with religion and morality. Meditation is regarded as a method of making a personal link with a personal aspect of the deity. One has only to look through a dozen or so of the Catholic booklets for the laity containing instructions in the subject to be convinced of this. They are intended as schemes of devotional and moral training in the Christian faith.

Patanjali approaches the subject from an entirely different angle. He regards meditation as a method of training human consciousness in such a way that it can function at levels other than the ordinary, range through a wider compass. His method is comparable to one of voice-production, in which the trainer gives to the pupil certain exercises in order by degrees to enlarge the compass of the voice and make the vocal instrument flexible. After years of such training the pupil becomes a singer, and sings what he chooses. The modern method in all artistic training is along these lines. Children are no longer taught to paint set pictures, or to dance set dances. We train them from baby-hood in the principles of expressing a three-dimensional world by means of line and colour on a two-dimensional surface. Dancing, in the ordinary non-professional sense, is no longer a question of how to perform the fashionable steps of the day, but of training in the principles of movement and rhythm, so that a finished dancer can execute any step or variant with facility and ease. Similarly in other branches of educational training—history is no longer a matter of dates, wars, and kings, but of facility in dealing with social and economic factors; geography is not a question of capes and bays, counties and capitals, but of learning to understand how factors of climate, relief, and vegetation combine to produce any given type of human life and settlement. This is simply to say that the whole trend of western education in the present day is toward producing increased capacity to deal with any given type of material, rather than toward building up familiarity with any special section of material.

Similarly yoga is not a training in the tenets of any religious faith, but an exercising of the spiritual faculty of man, an expansion of his capacity to deal with spiritual reality in whatever form. Hence the yoga sutras neither set forth a religious dogma nor inculcate any form of morality as such. Patanjali does not say, 'abstain from drink because drunkenness is wicked, attain continence because incontinence is a sin'. His attitude toward such things is that of the athletic trainer rather than of the moralist. Certain habits are inimical to the state of consciousness which is being sought, just as certain habits are inconsistent with physical fitness. This non-moral attitude of yoga, while wholly consonant with sound psychological practice in the west, is a great stumbling-block to many western minds in more ways than one. Such readers—I am of course not speaking of the experienced oriental student—approach a yoga treatise with the idea that since a yogi is 'an Indian holy man', therefore yoga must be a religious study, and must of necessity involve a standard of morality and also some definite dogma. From our standpoint of religion and morality the yoga sutras are both redundant and deficient. They enjoin various practices that are in western eyes foolish, irrelevant, inconvenient and unnecessary; and appear to ignore much that we consider vital. Thus in the four books of Patanjali only four or five sutras are concerned with devotion to a personal deity, and these merely recommend it as a useful practice, as one way of expanding spiritual capacity. On the other hand abstinence from flesh food and from all forms of alcoholic drink is assumed as a *sine qua non*. To such a restriction we may perhaps reply that our climate and mode of life are such that we need flesh foods and stimulating drinks. 'Possibly' says the yogi 'that may be so; and in that case to practise yoga in northern Europe is perhaps not feasible.' To him no moral controversy is involved, nor is he desirous of converting any one. These are simply the rules of the game. No one need play the game unless he wishes to do so.

But though there is little or no space given, particularly in the first three books, to philosophical questions, a great deal of philosophy is assumed; and as much of this is foreign to the western mind we must pause here to consider these assumptions if we are to have an adequate background on which to evaluate the yoga sutras themselves.

Eastern philosophy as a whole accepts the idea of the endless continuity of existence. Evolution not only of form but of consciousness is taken for granted. This means that to the Darwinian picture of the evolution of the complex from the simple in terms of physical structure there is added the idea of an evolving consciousness, at first vague and instinctual, but gradually becoming more alert, responsive and specialized, and by its own development compelling the evolution of new and subtler physical vehicles for its expression. The potentialities of this expanding life are illimitable: hence the future of the human race is to all intents unpredictable. This conception of the gradual evolution of consciousness involves for the Hindu a vast time scheme. The origin of the human race is placed in a much earlier geological age than that accepted by the western geologist. The Hindu has therefore a different standard of measurement as regards the progress of human evolution.

There are six great schools of Indian philosophy, ranging from pure materialism, with matter the determining factor, to the mysticism of the vedanta; but only two, the sankhya and the vedanta, need concern us here.

The sankhya has for its fundamental concept the idea that the universe is a duality. Purusha, spirit, is eternal, and prakriti, matter, is co-eternal with spirit. Purusha and prakriti are inseparable and are inherent in the manifested universe. Prakriti has three modes or aspects, rajas or activity, tamas or inertia, and sattva, rhythm or balance. These three, called the three gunas, combine in an infinite variety of manifestations which constitute the universe, and the student will notice recurrent trinities of classification due to this underlying conception of the threefold nature of matter.

There are two variants of sankhya philosophy, one which is entirely atheistic, and the other which accepts the idea of a deity, Ishvara. This last is usually called the 'sankhya with God', and is followed by Patanjali.

The vedanta philosophy accepts the sankhyan cosmogony, but cannot rest content with the duality of spirit and matter, purusha and prakriti. It seeks the cause of the manifested universe in the unmanifest and formless Brahman, and holds that all but Brahman is maya, illusion. All that changes is illusory, and the One that is permanent is the only reality, the changeless substratum beneath all appearances.

Thus these two great schools of Indian philosophy are at issue as to whether there exists a Supreme Being, an entity corresponding to the Christian concept of God, while they are united as regards the immortality of the soul and the continuity of existence. Here we get a position exactly the converse of that which exists in Europe, for the majority of Europeans who are interested in the non-material aspects of human existence are united by a belief in a supreme God, but are divided on questions pertaining to the continuity of existence.

In the yoga sutras Patanjali accepts as axiomatic the idea of the continuous existence of the individual human being, who is assumed to have had other lives before the life in which he studies yoga and who envisages further lives ahead; but he suggests to his students that they accept the idea of God as merely the most convenient hypothesis. This point of view is to him essentially logical.

He holds that the entire universe is part of a vast evolutionary scheme, that every human being passes through life after life, slowly progressing by an age-long process of evolution through rebirth toward ineffable heights of spiritual perfection. He envisages for every man an ultimate literal realization of Christ's dictum 'Be ye perfect'. From this it follows that there must exist at any given time not only those below us in achievement, but in an ascending scale beings so infinitely higher than ourselves as to be, from our angle of vision, gods. While recognizing these and regarding them as objects of devotion, Patanjali would assume that at our present stage and with our limited mental capacities we are essentially unable to give any final answer to the question of whether or no there does exist a Supreme Being. There are obviously 'gods many and lords many', but he sees human intellect as incapable of any final pronouncement on the nature or being of the Ultimate Entity. Yet, as the scientist adopts some vast and remote hypothesis to supply a convenient working basis, so for the student of yoga it is useful to hypothecate the existence of God; because such an hypothesis gives a focus, is as it were a pulley ring on which the weight of consciousness can be lifted. Here again we have a reversal of values as between east and west. The western mystic sets high value on one-pointedness because it leads the soul to God; the eastern yogi sets high value on the conception of God because it leads to one-pointedness. Scattered and diffused states of consciousness are inimical to progress in yoga, recollectedness is the fundamental requisite.

The vedantist who wishes to practise yoga has no objection whatsoever to using the rules of Patanjali. The fact that the sankhyan philosopher is by literal definition an atheist does not shock his religious sense, any more than the non-acceptance of the Einstein theory would shock ours. The existence or non-existence of a supreme deity is a fundamental question in philosophy and is accepted as the basic difference between the sankhya and the vedanta, but it is not regarded as fundamental for spiritual and religious development. In the east it is not only possible but common for a man who does not in our sense of the word 'believe in God' to devote his entire life to spiritual exercises that we should describe as prayer. The explanation of this apparent contradiction is that he does believe in human evolution, and is moreover prepared to give what the west would call worship to a human being very greatly in advance of himself, on somewhat the same terms as the west gives it to the divinely human personality of Christ. The Christian, and more especially the Teutonic Christian, has a profound racial instinct that the true eastern

lacks, one which presents him with a whole series of
religious and moral problems that do not exist for
the Hindu. The people of northern Europe are
strongly monotheistic and have accepted the first
and second commandments of the Jewish decalogue
whole-heartedly, embedding them in the very mat-
rix of their religious thought. The Protestant Christian would feel a sense of guilt in offering worship to
Christ Himself save for the fact that he regards Him
as being 'equal to the Father as touching His God-
head'. The eastern lacks this urge toward mono-
theism. He conceives of a divine hierarchy of highly
evolved beings to any and all of whom he is prepared to give worship in their degree, accepting the
fact that some are more lofty than others but feeling no personal concern about it, no responsibility
for adjudicating degrees of divinity. To him the
great need is dedication to something higher than
the personal self—but to each man his own conception of who or what that something may be.

Another idea accepted by Patanjali as axiomatic
is what might be called the cosmic law of cause and
effect, or the law of karma. According to this
conception chance is non-existent. Every circumstance, every smallest happening has had its cause
in the past and will have its result in the future.
Man in the earlier stages of his evolution is under
this iron law, 'bound to the wheel' as Kim's lama

has it. He cannot escape the results of the past and must again and again meet the results of mistakes made in past lives until he learns to deal with similar situations adequately—that is creatively rather than automatically. 'Forgiveness of sin' in the sense of exemption from the consequences of sin has no place in eastern philosophy. But this law also involves the fact that by his actions man can control his future, for he can create in the present what will produce the desired effect. In his earlier phases, however, his ignorance is such that he does not see how to control the future, or if he sees lacks the necessary trick of self-mastery. There is moreover a method of mastering karma completely, of being in a position to make of it a tool rather than a fetter. If man can succeed in disentangling himself entirely from desire, so that never at any time does he act or choose under its impulsion, but always from right knowledge of circumstances and deliberate will in accordance with that knowledge—if, as we would say in western parlance, he can become psychologically free—then he is lord of the fields of human experience, loosed from the bondage of his karma for ever. To attain this freedom is the goal of human evolution.

Many of the sutras in the first two books of Patanjali relate to the means of working toward this goal, and a real understanding of the profound philosophy involved in the eastern idea of karma, or the law of cause and effect governing states of consciousness as well as physical conditions, is essential if one is to grasp his meaning.

It is our custom to regard this philosophy of karma as one of indolent easy-going fatalism, and to attribute to it many of the evils of eastern social life. It is in reality the complete negation of fatalism in that it deletes chance, 'destiny' in the colloquial acceptance of the word, and the idea of an 'over-ruling providence'—all three fairly common conceptions in the west. It represents man as the sole and absolute master of his own fate for ever. What he has sown in the time of his ignorance he must inevitably reap, but when he attains enlightenment it is for him to sow what he chooses and reap accordingly.

In the west we have attained some degree of understanding of the importance of the law of cause and effect in the physical world. The whole history of scientific discovery is one of patient research into this law as applied to physical phenomena. It is recognized that when a scientific experiment is uncertain in its results this is due to some unknown factor, and not to accident—to man's ignorance, not to nature's unreliability or to an 'act of God'. We are all familiar with articles of commerce which are unreliable in quality because they are made by an imperfect process, i.e. a process in which cause and effect are not as yet completely understood. In the psychological and spiritual worlds of experience we have scarcely as yet even begun to explore the working of this law. Probably the largest factor in the make-up of the human race at its present stage of evolution is the emotional nature. The news that fills nine-tenths of the penny papers would be non-existent were it not for the emotions of love, hate, jealousy, greed, lust, vanity, courage, ambition, and the like. And what do we really know about cause and effect in the emotional world? Why have some people strong emotions and others not? Why does A fall in love with B and not with C? Why is sexual passion usually short-lived? And why not always? Why is jealousy the commonest of the vices? Is there a reliable method by which a human being can evoke in himself any specified emotion? If so, how does it work? Exactly how does anger affect (*a*) the author, (*b*) the recipient? Why does an outburst of temper refresh and relieve some people and upset and deplete others?

The replies that we are able to make to this kind of question are pitiably inadequate, and hence the world of emotion seems to us to be governed very largely by chance. For a long time we have realized dimly that there is a relation between emotion and disease—certain habitual emotional states have been suspected of being at least a contributory cause of certain diseases. But this field of research has scarcely been approached except by the analyst, and even he has touched but the fringe of it as yet.

The eastern doctor, whose knowledge of the physical body appears to us at times so unscientific, has nevertheless for centuries been aware of a profound relation between emotional states and disease, and his medical training begins with a study of how to purify and control the desires and emotions. He is taught to investigate the state of his patient's feelings before attacking his physical symptoms. Similarly the eastern psychologist has far more to say of a definite and schematic nature about the mind and emotions of man, and the law of cause and effect in relation to them, than ourselves. To any of the questions that I have suggested above he has a clear and complete answer which satisfies him because it is based upon experiments which he can verify for himself and which have been constantly verified by others. They are so familiar to the eastern mind that they can be stated in axiomatic form, and Patanjali accepts these axioms of emotional and mental experience and bases his instruction on them. To him there is no such thing as chance, for he regards the law of cause and effect as universal, immutable, and applicable to the psychological as well as to the physical field.

Yet another conception which is like a continuous thread running through the sutras is that of form at super-physical levels. This is an outcome or corollary of the sankhyan theory of purusha and prakriti, spirit and matter, and of the three gunas (see p. 80). The European can readily enough grasp the idea that the physical universe is a manifestation of spirit and matter in innumerable and indissoluble combinations, because he is aware of that mysterious something called 'life' which permeates all things; but it is to him a staggering improbability that the interior experiences of emotion, thought and will possess at their own level suitable forms, forms which are substantial to the perception of those levels of experience. To the westerner the idea that a feeling or a thought has spatial existence is merely funny, whereas to the Hindu it is an everyday fact. To the European the dictum 'thoughts are things' suggests a crank religion; to the Hindu it is a platitude. He sees man as able to function in various states of consciousness differing from one another not in kind so much as in rate of vibration. All experiences consist of activities of spirit-matter of varying degrees of density, and the response of consciousness to this stimulus. Thus feelings and thoughts exist in space, have a shape, a rate of movement, and a period of duration. It has been said by a well-known European scholar deeply versed in Hindu philosophy that the failure of the western student to grasp this idea of spatial extension as applied to thought and emotion is the great stumbling-block to his comprehension of eastern philosophical ideas.

Still one further concept of the eastern psychologist must be considered in connexion with the yoga sutras, namely that of states of consciousness. The idea of thoughts and emotions as having objective existence may be strange to the west, but most of us can verify for ourselves by a little introspection the fact that the ordinary man is aware of himself at three levels, the physical, the emotional, and the mental, with a faint overshadowing of true volition. Thus it is possible to be conscious more or less simultaneously of physical cold, of emotional depression, and of some such mental activity as adding up figures, drawing a ground-plan, or arranging a railway journey. The consciousness is at any given moment *focused* on one of these planes, but the other two are in the periphery. These are the worlds in which we commonly live, but in the east they are three worlds, not two. Emotion is not regarded as merely a mode of thought, though in waking life thought and feeling work in close combination.

Again, emotion has a very much wider connotation to the Hindu than to us. To him the child's dislike of bitter medicine, the adult's craving for wine, are as much part of the emotional state as the murderer's hatred of his victim. All desire and all aversion belong to this range of experience, the wish-world of Freud; and in so far as a man is under the dominance of kama,[1] desire, and so allows his activities to be governed by his automatic attractions and repulsions, he is still an infant in the game of life.

The eastern psychologist has taught for centuries that emotion is dual in nature, is in fact a pendulum swing of consciousness from the extreme of liking to the extreme of disliking.[2] This duality of experience in the emotional field is beginning to be noted nowadays among experimental psychologists in the west. Pain-pleasure, attraction-aversion are found to be linked experiences, with a tendency on the part of the individual to react from one into its extreme opposite.

Mental consciousness is regarded as being definitely of two kinds. The mental faculties which develop in childhood, more or less concurrently with the emotions, are those of concrete thought, the whole range that is commonly used in carrying on the objective thinking and the ordinary activities of daily life. Any adult who is not

---

[1] *Kama*, desire, is to be distinguished from *karma*, which literally means action.　　　　[2] See *Science of the Emotions*, Bhagavan Das.

mentally deficient functions freely in this state, which is always more or less highly coloured by emotion.

The subtler mental faculties, which are regarded as closely allied to spiritual consciousness and beyond the range of personal emotion, comprise all abstract thought, all creative activity. Such thinking is the field of experience in which the artist, the philosopher, the mathematician are at home, but it is scarcely touched by the average unintelligent man or by the young child. Spearman and his school seem to have isolated this faculty and term it 'insight'. It is defined as the capacity for being able to call up a greater variety and number of correlates to any given idea or stimulus, and enables the fortunate possessor to react with 'originality' to given situations.

The Hindu conception of will is comparable to that of many western philosophers and psychologists,[1] but bears little relation to the unscientific and colloquial use of the word by the generality of people. We are accustomed to say that a man has a strong will when he is capable of making a clear mental picture of a desired objective and holding it clinched and rigid at all costs. Thus the father with a fixed idea that his son shall ultimately enter the family business or profession, who sticks to it re-

[1] Cf. *ABC of Adler's Psychology*, by Mairet.

gardless of the talents and proclivities which the child develops, is said to be strong-willed, although in a sense we realize that he is merely too self-satisfied to destroy his own fantasy. Coué's famous dictum that when the will and the imagination are in conflict the imagination always conquers is based on the popular idea of will, and as a result the general public who read Coué, while they felt something to be wrong with the statement, could never refute it. The classic example is that of the man who determines to get up at six o'clock, and when he is called allows his imagination to picture the cold and discomfort of dressing as against the warmth and ease of bed. In such a case, says Coué, the 'will' to get up always gives way to the imagination of discomfort. But in reality the conflict is not between will and imagination but between two incompatible desires. The man desires for some reason to get up early—pleasure, ambition, self-esteem may be his motive —and he makes a mind-picture of the *desirability* of getting up. When the time comes this conflicts with the mind-picture of the *desirability* of bed, and a struggle ensues in which one desire becomes stronger than the other and wins. The trouble is not that will has been defeated, but that it has never come into play. The state of consciousness has been purely a conflict of mento-emotional associations and of motives, and true volition has not been touched. The Hindu conceives of will (atma) as being a state of consciousness transcending thought and feeling, an impersonal or non-emotional experience. In so far as the ordinary man uses it at all it is a function of deletion, of inhibition. By its means the picture-making faculty itself can be checked, the back-and-forth of the concrete mind can be stilled, and the hidden intention, the thing that the self really wants, brought into effect. Decisions can be made which are contrary to desire, contrary to personal interest. These impinge upon ordinary life, bringing into it a new type of power. This view of will can be paralleled in western experimental psychology, for the personalists, after long research into the nature of choice, describe all acts of volition as involving a reference to the self, a calling upon something other than the picture-making faculty. They do not all agree as to what that self may be, but they do agree that volition is one of its functions.

One of the reasons why will and desire are so frequently confused is that the same outward result may be produced by the victory of the more violent desire as by the use of will. While the disinclination to get up can be downed by a heated struggle in which the imagination pictures in glowing colours the advantage to be gained by rising immediately, the same result can also be brought about by deleting all pictures, by acting at once and not stopping to think. In the latter case the will works quickly and smoothly, and without the struggle involved in the former method. In the first case the lock is as it were forced, in the other the mechanism is placed in perfect alignment and the key turns noiselessly. Though the result is the same the mechanisms involved are utterly dissimilar.

To sum up what has been said about states of consciousness—the Hindu philosopher recognizes five such states, the physical, emotional, mental (mind being regarded as dual, see diagram p. 97), spiritual or intuitional, and volitional. The ordinary man in his workaday hours functions normally in three of these—he has physical and emotional and concrete mental consciousness easily at his command. By a momentary effort, or more continuously if he has been habituated to it by education and circumstances, he can touch the region of insight or creative thought which is closely linked with the intuitional or spiritual state. Volitional consciousness is extremely rare at this stage of human evolution, for though man does use his will he is seldom able to use it with awareness. To illustrate this rather difficult idea by means of a comparison—man uses his digestive powers to deal with his food, but he is not able to direct them, and by giving the digestive process his conscious attention he tends to hinder and not to help it. Similarly he possesses and uses in everyday life a faculty or capacity of will, but he is not really aware of its mechanism. It is a flick of consciousness that comes into play he knows not how. Deliberate thought retards it, spiritual aspiration sometimes quickens it.

From the above it may be seen that the east has a definite contribution to make on the subject of will, and of this more is to be said. At the moment let us return to a consideration of the fivefold classification. Emotion, according to the eastern idea, includes all reaction to sensations and all feelings, and hence the emotional scale is very extensive in range. Its more primitive manifestations are interlocked with the physical, its higher phases are mingled with thought. Thus the pleasure of a warm bath, the pain of a jambed finger, represent emotion linked to the body but scarcely related to thought; whereas the pleasure of reading an entertaining story and the pain of anxiety lest your wife may have been involved in a motor accident have very little physical element, but are, as it were, a chemical compound of thought and emotion. In other words these five states of consciousness have to be pictured not as consecutive, but as overlapping, in a way that is roughly illustrated by the accompanying diagram.

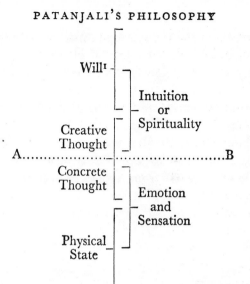

The states of consciousness shown in the diagram above the line A—B represent the Hindu idea of what we call the immortal soul, or the spirit—that which survives death, the ego, the self. Those below the line represent a reflection of the self, its behaviour and appearance in everyday life, what Jung would call the persona. Throughout the sutras of Patanjali we meet constantly with this conception of the self abiding in its own nature and yet partially entangled in the world of phenomenal experience,

---

[1] The diagram shows will as extending beyond intuition, and the physical below the range of sensation. This is strictly in accordance with Eastern metaphysic, but not relevant to the present discussion.

the Seer (See-er) identifying himself with the seen. To disentangle the Seer from the seen, the self from its personal experience, is set forth as the goal of yoga.

These axiomatic philosophical conceptions on which the sutras of Patanjali are based have been touched on very slightly in the above pages, but as they form the substratum of a great deal of what is to follow, they will from time to time recur and be considered.

Chapter VII

THE YOGA SUTRAS OF PATANJALI

THE problem of making a comparison between yoga and analytical therapy is rendered difficult by the fact that very few western readers are acquainted with the Yoga Sutras,[1] and that those who do read them find them for the most part incomprehensible. There exist several English translations, but where these have been made by Hindus the phraseology used is very misleading to the European reader, and where they have been made by English students the endeavour to render them intelligible has often led to a very wide departure from the original.

As it is essential to my purpose that the substance of the sutras should be accessible to my readers, I have ventured to make a paraphrase of the four books or chapters of Patanjali. This paraphrase does not pretend to be an accurate translation or even an authoritative rendering, but merely a careful interpretation of one aspect of their meaning. That they have other and deeper meanings I am fully aware.

[1] The word *sutra* means 'a collection of rules'; but it has been anglicized by long usage, and applied to the separate verses of a collection.

THE SUTRAS
BOOK I

1.[1] *Now an exposition of Yoga is to be made.*

2.   *Yoga is attained by gaining complete mastery over the mind and emotions.*

3.   *The individual then becomes aware of himself.*

4.   *Ordinarily he is identified with or lost in his own confused picture of life.*

COMMENT. Sutras 2 and 3 state the fundamental thesis of the science of yoga. Ordinarily a man is lost in his own confused thought and feeling, but when yoga is attained the personal consciousness becomes stilled 'like a lamp in a windless place', and it is then possible for the embodied spirit to know itself as apart from the manifestations to which it is accustomed, and to become aware of its own nature. This thesis obviously involves the whole philosophical position of the sankhya theory of the universe. As has been stated, purusha and prakriti, spirit and matter, life and form, are regarded as interdependent; and just as in Christian dogma spirit does not exclude the idea of spirits or souls, so here purusha is one and fundamental, and yet there are purushas or individual spirits, linked to forms provided by the form-building principle or prakriti. These forms are manifestations of the three gunas, the three types of energy which are the

[1] I have followed Dvivedi's numbering of the sutras.

three aspects of prakriti—tamas or inertia, rajas or activity, and sattva or rhythm. It should be noted that the idea of form as energy manifesting in a given way is wholly familiar to present-day science.

The gunas are active at every level of personal consciousness, physical, emotional, and mental. They are automatic, and when linked to an individual purusha or human soul they give it vast and varied experience but tend to blind it to its own true nature. This is discussed in Book II, sutras 17–25, and in Book IV, sutras 31–4.

5–6. *The activities or states of the personal consciousness are five. It may be engaged in clear thinking, in confused thinking, in fancy, in sleep, or in memory.*

7. *Right knowledge is obtained by direct observation, or by the use of reliable information, or by accurate inference from either of these sources.*

8. *Confused thinking is a false conception of a thing whose real form does not correspond to that conception.*

9. *Fancy is a notion founded on a knowledge conveyed by words alone, and having no object corresponding to it in reality.*

COMMENT. Some commentators imply that fancy partakes of the nature of verbal delusion, as even after discerning the absurdity involved in a verbal expression not in accordance with fact, people yet deal with it as if it were actually based on sense perception. It depends on circumstances whether any serious error results from this or not; for example, we say the sun rises and sets, but no serious harm results from the use of this 'fancy'.

Fantasy, as the western psychologist employs the term to-day, would fall under the head of confused thinking; but actual delusions come under the head of fancy rather than of fantasy.

10. *Sleep is the automatic withdrawal of consciousness from the external.*

COMMENT. The trained yogi can induce this condition by will, in which case it is called trance.

11. *Memory is a right recollection of experience.*

12–13. *Yoga is attained by the control and ultimately the suppression at will of all forms of thinking, and is gained by determined and sustained effort coupled with increasing detachment and dispassion.*

14. *At first it is achieved spasmodically, but in time and with steady effort it becomes an habitual state.*

COMMENT. The sutras from 15 to the end of Book I are concerned with definite stages or phases of consciousness which result from the practice of yoga. They are difficult for us to understand because we are unaccustomed to such definiteness in regard to states of consciousness. In order that the next thirty-seven sutras may convey some meaning to the western reader I propose to indicate in brief what these states are.

Samādhi, or meditation, is of two kinds, conscious and unconscious. The object of the yogi is to attain to unconscious samādhi, and this is done by strenuous practice of conscious samādhi.

Conscious samādhi is characterized by the fact that in it there is consciousness of the thinker and the thought as being apart. There are four stages of conscious samādhi.

I. The first stage is concerned with objects and sense impressions. In this stage, as in the other three, there are two modes of concentration, known as the argumentative and the non-argumentative. These two modes are fairly easily understood by the ordinary student in so far as they affect the lower stages of samādhi. Thus, in concentrating on some object such as a seed, it is possible to consider its attributes and to let the mind move round it and form ideas and inferences about it. This is argumentative concentration. It is further possible, with practice, to hold the mind perfectly still on the object, without making any statements or inferences about it. This is non-argumentative concentration, and can be sustained by the untrained mind for a brief moment only.

II. The second stage of samādhi is concerned not with objects and sense impressions, but with causes and ideas lying behind external phenomena.

III. The third stage is concerned with the gunas (see p. 80) and especially with sattva, i.e. rhythm or equilibrium. This is called joyous meditation, because to attain a purely sattvic or rhythmic state of consciousness is to be in a state of joy. Sattva is regarded as the cause which enables the senses to perform their functions, and hence this form of samādhi is said to be an exercise in cognizing the instrument of cognition.

Those who succeed in mastering fully this third stage are said to be *videha*, or free from the bonds of matter.

IV. The fourth stage is concerned with purusha, the cause of all causes, the knower. The yogi in this stage is no longer conscious of the known, but only of the knower, and is very close to the goal of unconscious samādhi. He is said to be *prakritilaya*, i.e. he is free in prakriti or dissolved in prakriti; but he has not achieved his goal, which is to rise beyond prakriti or to escape the bondage of the activities of the material universe.

Beyond these four stages of conscious samādhi, which are regarded as means to an end, lies unconscious samādhi, a state of pure purusha or pure being in which there is bliss and freedom, but no objective consciousness of knower or known.

15. *When complete disentanglement from the phenomenal world is attained, then non-attachment has been reached.*

16. *A still higher condition of consciousness is attainable wherein nothing exists other than purusha.*

17. *There are four stages of conscious samādhi concerned respectively with external phenomena, with the causes of phenomena, with rhythm or joy, and with the sense of being or purusha.*

18. *The next stage involves the suspension of all mental activity.* (i.e. Unconscious samādhi.)

19. *The person who attains to these forms of concentration[1] before arriving at complete detachment of spirit from the phenomenal world still has his thinking determined for him by the sequence of external phenomena. He becomes caged, or as one who has entered a burning building of which the stairs collapse behind him.*

COMMENT. That is to say, the yogi who attains to the third and fourth stages of conscious samādhi and goes no further is trapped, because he cannot return to the ordinary consciousness of mankind, and yet he has not reached his true goal.

20. *The student who intends to reach the goal of true detachment must be willing to sacrifice all other objectives, and must have energy, accurate memory of past experience, and discrimination.*

COMMENT. The insistence on 'memory' as a necessary qualification for yoga is noteworthy. The ancient commentaries on the sutras indicate that by memory is meant the capacity to recall past experience *as it really was*, free from glamour and emotional confusion. It will be recognized that to

[1] i.e. to the third and fourth stages of conscious samādhi.

attain this capacity is one of the main objects of analysis.

21. *Detachment is most rapidly attained by those who know how to use the will.*

22. *Some would-be students are but dabblers, some are serious in their efforts, but only the few are entirely one-pointed.*

23. *Among various ways of attaining yoga, one of the quickest is through complete devotion to God.*

24-5. *God is a spirit, untouched by human modifications, in whom is infinite that omniscience which in man is but a germ.*

26. *God is not limited by time.*

27. *The Sacred Word OM represents Him.*

28-9. *By concentrated reflection on the idea of God there comes a knowledge of Him and a gradual overcoming of the obstacles to yoga.*

30. *The obstacles in the way of the man who sets out to attain yoga are ill health, boredom, doubt, carelessness, laziness, worldly-mindedness, incapacity to perceive what is required, the tendency to be led off into side issues after a certain measure of success has been attained,[1] and inability to stay the course.*

31. *Pain, mental distress, nervous disorders, and irregular breathing accompany these obstacles or causes of distraction.*

[1] e.g. occasionally yoga practices develop in the student a certain degree of psychism (shown in clairvoyance, automatic writing, etc.) which may fascinate and distract him.

COMMENT. In yoga practice great importance is given to breathing, and this will be more fully discussed under sutras 46–55. To prevent the nervous conditions mentioned in sutra 31, and to steady the mind Patanjali suggests various means:

32. *Those may be prevented by steady and intense concentration on some subject.*

33. *Also by the deliberate practice of such attitudes of mind as sympathy, compassion, cheerfulness.*

34. *Or by the practice of prānayāmā, the science of breath.*

35–9. *Or by meditation upon any engrossing sensory experience, or upon an impersonal subject such as the quality of peace, or upon some divinely perfect being, or upon the experience obtained in dream and in sleep, or upon any deeply congenial subject.*

COMMENT. The yogi regards dreams as being significant, and considers that deep and dreamless sleep is not a blank, but contains useful experience for those who have the skill to understand it.

40. *The student whose mind is steadied by meditation obtains mastery which extends from the atomic to the infinite.*

41. *When the modifications of the mind have all been stilled, then the consciousness, like a pure crystal, takes the colour of what it rests on, whether that be the perceiver, the perceiving, or the thing perceived.*

COMMENT. The theory of understanding here pre-

sented is taken from vedanta teaching. Tookaram
Tatya says:

'The internal organ (i.e. the understanding principle)
is there compared to water, in respect of its readiness to
adapt itself to the form of whatever mould it may enter.
As the waters of a reservoir, having issued from an aper-
ture and having entered by a channel the basins, become
four-cornered or otherwise shaped just like them, so the
manifesting internal organ having gone through the sight
or other channel to where there is an object . . . becomes
modified by the form of the . . . object. This altered state
of the internal organ is called its modification. This
manifesting internal organ, whilst it is regarded as mould-
ing itself upon an object, is regarded as at the same time
manifesting it—or revealing it as a mirror does.'[1]

COMMENT. Sutras 42–51 deal with the four stages
of conscious samādhi and the final attainment of
unconscious samādhi. (See comment, pp. 103 et
seq.)

42. *In meditation that is concerned with external objects
    and sense impressions, the argumentative stage consists
    in thinking about the object and pondering its aspects
    and its meaning.*

43. *In the non-argumentative stage this associative pro-
    cess ceases, and there follows complete absorption in the
    idea itself.*

44. *The same two processes take place in meditation on
    causes and abstract ideas.*

[1] *Yoga Philosophy of Patanjali* (p. 6).

45. *In the two further stages of samādhi analytical thought is no longer possible.*

COMMENT. This sutra in the original is very obscure, but its general meaning is that in profound meditation thought is transcended.

46. *These forms of samādhi are conscious and are described as 'meditation with seed'.*

47. *In the highest stage of conscious samādhi there is complete absorption and contentment.*

48–9. *At this stage knowledge is gained by intuition and is completely reliable. The intuitive method is one of direct cognition, and is superior to that of inference and testimony.* (See sutra 7.)

50. *In this state of consciousness all ideas are gradually generalized into one, which is as a stationary spectacle before the spectator.*

51. *When the stationary spectacle is also removed, unconscious samādhi or meditation without seed is attained.* (See sutra 18.)

BOOK II

The first book of the Yoga Sutras having dealt in a general way with the subject of samādhi and the nature of the goal to be aimed at, the second proceeds to give rather detailed directions intended for those who wish to attain the goal but require preliminary training. For the western student this is the most significant and intelligible of the four books. It deals with two main subjects, namely the initial difficulties in the practice of yoga, and the relation between the soul or seer (i.e. that which sees) and the objective world. As before said, the basic idea of yoga is that the soul is immersed in the objective world, the eternal deeply entangled in the transient, the real in the unreal; and man's task is to disentangle himself in such a way that the soul becomes a spectator of the drama of his own experience. This disentanglement does not necessarily involve a withdrawal from active participation in life. It may take this form, but equally it may result in a state of 'recollectedness', to use the Christian term, in which the individual participates in life but is not immersed in it.

1–2. *The preliminary exercises for those who wish to practise yoga include discipline or relaxation of tension, study or aspiration, and resignation to God. These lead to the acquirement of habitual samādhi and to the overcoming of the obstacles thereto.*

COMMENT. The Sanskrit word here rendered as 'discipline' suggests the killing out of bondage to instinctual life, and is commonly translated as 'mortification'. Claude Bragdon[1] translates this as 'the discipline of the senses'. It refers immediately to the ordinary ascetic practices of fasts and pen-

[1] *Introduction to Yoga*, p. 86.

ances; but the underlying idea is that the student must by some means relax the emotional tension and ambivalence which holds him gripped to the external satisfactions and dissatisfactions of living.

By resignation to God is implied not so much devotion to a personal deity as an attitude of acceptance of life, obedience to the personal guru or teacher, and a willingness to sacrifice all other aims to the one aim, the attainment of liberation.

3. *Five obstacles stand in the way of attainment, viz. ignorance, sense of being or self-esteem, desire, aversion, and the will to live.*

4. *Ignorance is the cause of the other four. The five obstacles are suspended or dormant in the yogi who has attained to the higher stages of conscious samādhi; they are under control in the earnest student; they ebb and flow in the consciousness of the ordinary man.*

COMMENT. The idea is that the ordinary man is at the mercy of the obstacles, at one moment in the grip of a pleasurable sensation, at the next shaken by anger or distaste. Only in the highest state of unconscious samādhi are the obstacles transcended.

5. *Ignorance is a mental state in which the illusory is mistaken for reality, that which is apparent for the real.*

6. *Sense of being is the identification of the seer with the instruments of knowledge.*

COMMENT. The idea is that the true 'I', the ego, the

spirit, purusha, identifies itself habitually with the desires and with the physical body. The man who says 'I am hungry' means that his body is hungry. The spirit cannot be hungry. When he says 'I am angry', he is identifying the spirit with the emotional nature. It is this identification of purusha with the instruments of its manifestation, viz. senses emotions and mind, which causes a man to feel that his personal needs, his emotions of liking and disliking and his opinions are of supreme importance and urgency. Therefore sense of being is often rendered as self-assertion, self-esteem, egotism.

For the reader with some knowledge of Sanskrit terminology it is worth noting that this sense of being is not *ahankāra*, but *asmitā*. Ahankāra is a sense of self attained in the highest stages of conscious samādhi.[1]

7. *Desire is the dwelling on pleasure.*[2]

8. *Aversion is the dwelling on pain.*

9. *The will to live is universal, deeply embedded in all life.*

COMMENT. The ancient commentators say of the will to live: 'It is a feeling from which none is free, from the lowest worm to the highest sage; nay, even so-called inanimate nature is not free from it. It is

---

[1] Dvivedi, p. 10.
[2] cf. Lust is the resting in the sense of enjoyment : *The Yoga Sutras of Patanjali*, by Charles Johnston.

not produced in beings by education or example, but is purely innate.'[1]

10. *The latent seeds of these obstacles are eradicated only when the student has reached his goal.*

11. *The actual manifestation of the obstacles can be prevented by intentness of the mind on some one thing.* (See I. 32.)

12. *The obstacles are to be overcome because they are the source of karma and hence of rebirth.*

COMMENT. It is because a man longs for pleasure and fears pain, feels his own personal importance and has an intense desire to live, that all his actions, good and bad, are performed; and hence he piles up reactions to his actions, i.e. karma, which necessitate rebirth and fresh experience. This experience will be pleasurable or painful according to the actions which have occasioned it, but—and at this point the eastern view is very foreign to the western mind—whether the results of actions are pleasurable or painful their automatic recurrence is *equally* to be avoided.

13. *The karma of past actions is unavoidable and affects caste, length of life, and pleasantness or painfulness of experience.*

14. *Whether karma is pleasurable or painful depends on the nature of the acts that caused it.*

15. *But to the enlightened all rebirth is misery.*

[1] Dvivedi, p. 32.

16. *Although the student is not able to avoid the consequence of his previous actions, he will, in proportion as he gains insight, refrain from manufacturing fresh causes.*

17. *The basic cause of all karma is the identification of the self with experience and environment.*

COMMENT. At this point the writer diverges from the consideration of preliminary yoga training and enters upon a brief philosophical discussion of the relation between the self and the external world, the seer and the seen, purusha and prakriti.

18. *The seen, the phenomenal universe, whether visible to the eyes or invisible, is the result of the interaction of three forces,[1] motion, inertia, and poise or rhythm. The interweaving of these builds the elements and organs of nature which exist for the sake of spirit, purusha, and are the means of the evolution of consciousness.*

COMMENT. These elements and organs are elaborately studied in the sankhya philosophy. They are twenty-five in number, and are called the tattvas.

19. *These three forces are inherent at all levels of consciousness.*

COMMENT. This sutra has direct reference to the four stages of conscious samādhi, and indicates that the gunas are not transcended in any of those four states. It also refers in general to the spatial reality of thought and emotion. (See Ch. VI.)

_____
[1] i.e. the gunas-rajas, tamas, sattva.

20. *The seer, purusha, exists as pure capacity for awareness, but appears to use the intellect as a means of contacting experience*

21. *Nature has no ulterior purpose of her own. The only reason for her existence is the perception of her by the seer.*

22. *Yet there is objective reality in the universe, for it is the common source of all experience, and does not cease to exist because one soul ceases to be bound by it.*

23. *The self-identification of the seer with phenomenal experience is inherent in the nature of things. Although it is the cause of the obstacles, yet it is necessary in order to kindle the spark of self-consciousness into full activity.*

24. *Man's unconsciousness of his real nature, i.e. his state of ignorance, is the cause of this identification.*

25. *The goal to be aimed at is the destruction of ignorance by right knowledge. Its attainment constitutes complete liberation (i.e. kaivalya).*

26. *The means of attainment is ever-increasing discrimination.*

27. *During the process of attaining to liberation there is a sevenfold enlightenment.*

COMMENT. This sevenfold enlightenment is not explained in the sutras, but its nature is well known to eastern students. It is explained by Dvivedi as being a cessation of the following states of mind: (1) desire for knowledge; (2) desire for freedom; (3) desire for bliss; (4) desire to do one's duty;

(5) sorrow; (6) fear; (7) doubt. It might be described as the final expulsion of the sense of inferiority, of fear, and of insecurity.

From this point the writer returns to a direct consideration of preliminary yoga.

28. *By practising the preliminary exercises comes enlightenment, since the overcoming of the obstacles leads to the attainment of discrimination.*

29. *These preliminary exercises are:*

(1) *The practice of harmlessness, i.e. obedience to the moral law.*

(2) *Discipline, i.e. obedience to the spiritual law.*

(3) *Posture.*

(4) *The regulation of breath.*

(5) *Withdrawal or abstraction.*

(6) *Concentration.*

(7) *Deliberation.*

(8) *Contemplation.*

COMMENT. The first five of these exercises are dealt with in Book II, the last three in Book III. Of these eight the first five constitute a discipline of life, and the last three are actual meditation exercises or stages. Each of these eight exercises is elaborated in subsequent sutras.

30. *The moral law includes abstention from killing, lying, stealing, incontinence, and covetousness or greed.*

31. *This law is of universal obligation.*

32. *The spiritual discipline consists of purification, con-*

tentment, mortification or discipline, study and resignation to God. (See II. 1.)

33-4. *In order to eradicate undesirable thoughts, habits of mind, and emotions, the student is recommended to meditate upon their opposite. Their eradication is valuable not only because it makes for progress in yoga, but also because such thoughts produce misery.*

COMMENT. The next section of the sutras of Book II treats in detail of the results of self-training in the five stages of preliminary discipline. As regards obedience to the moral law, it is assumed that the yogi, like the Christian saint, interprets this law in the sense of the Sermon on the Mount and not in that of the Mosaic Commandments. Thus non-killing means complete and universal kindliness, non-lying and non-stealing imply an honesty and truth of crystalline clarity in all relations to life.

35. *When the student has acquired perfect kindliness, all beings, men and animals and birds, approach him without fear or reserve.*

36. *The truth-dealing man tends to draw truthfulness from those about him in subtler and subtler degrees, until a true thought becomes effective at its own level.*

37. *When avidity for possessions is overcome he receives in abundance at all levels.*

38. *Perfected continence gives vigour and creative capacity.*

39. *When desirelessness is attained, there comes an*

*understanding of the plan of life and the reason for
existence.*

COMMENT. That is to say that the man who lets go
his clutch on life understands life.[1]

40–1. *Spiritual discipline also has its appropriate results:
through purity of body and mind comes a true perception
of relationships, a ceasing from infatuation with bodily
intercourse, a surmounting of all loneliness, which makes
possible communion with the soul (purusha).*

42. *From contentment the student gains supreme happiness.*

COMMENT. Contentment, i.e. acceptance of conditions, acceptance of other people as they are, and of
himself.

43. *From discipline—i.e. one-pointed willingness to sacrifice all for an end—there come spiritual capacity and
occult powers.*

44. *From study or fervent aspiration there arises a link
with the deity.*

45. *By subordinating the personal will entirely to the
interior will perfection in samādhi is achieved.*

COMMENT. The concluding sutras of Book II are
in their obvious interpretation concerned with the
technical yoga postures of the body and breathing
exercises. In the east, where these postures and
exercises are commonly practised and found very
beneficial by all serious students of yoga, it is this
aspect of the sutras that is usually emphasized by

[1] Cf. 'He that loveth his life shall lose it' (John xii. 25).

writers and commentators. They have, however, an obvious further application of still greater importance.

46. *An easy and steady bodily position is necessary for prolonged meditation.*

47. *A suitable posture should be acquired by gradual effort, and when it has been acquired the mind can then be detached for its true work.*

48. *The fruit of right poise is the capacity to remain balanced between the pairs of opposites.*

49. *When this is gained there follows the right guidance of the life currents, the control of the incoming and outgoing breath.*[1]

50-5. *These sutras deal with the science of breath-control known as prānayāma, and the results thereby attained.*

COMMENT. The word prāna implies to the eastern student much more than breath. It is the vital energy that is in all forms, and may be termed life-force. Its most obvious manifestation in the human physical body is the motion of the lungs. The student of yoga is taught that by scientific control of the life-force or prāna in the body, i.e. by the regulation of the breath, it is possible to obtain mastery over deep-seated forces in consciousness as well as in external nature. The process has been very much elaborated and those who wish for details can find them in *The Mysterious Kundalini* by Dr. Rele and *The Serpent*

---

[1] This translation follows that of Johnston.

Power by Sir John Woodroffe. For our purpose it is sufficient to say that breath is first made rhythmic and then suspended, the latter condition inducing trance in extreme instances.

During the training in breath-control the student is instructed how to withdraw his consciousness from sense contacts, sight, hearing, etc., so that it remains suspended in a condition of pure thinking without an object. It will be noted that this process is parallel to the description given of the four stages of conscious samādhi. Prānayāma is a technical aid to the attainment of the higher stages of samādhi. A warning is almost invariably given that exercises in prānayāma demand the help of an experienced teacher.

BOOK III

INTRODUCTORY COMMENT

This book deals entirely with the last three of the eight preliminary exercises enumerated in Book II, sutra 29, namely concentration, deliberation, contemplation, and with the results which are to be obtained by practising them.

These three exercises are called respectively dharana, dhyana, and samādhi, and the term samyāma is used to designate the three collectively considered. Their practice leads to the state called conscious samādhi, and hence they are sometimes called exercises in conscious samādhi.

Sutra.

1. *Concentration is holding the attention fixed upon an object.*
2. *Sustained concentration upon one object is deliberation.*

COMMENT. The implication of this sutra in the original is that the mind takes on the shape of the object of deliberation. For the understanding of many of these sutras it is important constantly to remember the eastern conception of thought (mind) as being a subtle type of energy capable of building up forms. The western student is apt to regard these statements about mind as metaphorical when they are in fact intended to be taken literally.

3. *When all consciousness is lost save that of the shape on which the mind is fixed, this state is contemplation.*

COMMENT. This third stage is regarded by the commentators as a somewhat dangerous one, since it may easily lead to mediumistic trance. (See further note on sutra 8.)

These three stages of concentration are clearly distinguished in Sanskrit by three definite terms, which to the eastern mind have a scientific accuracy. Western mystics have recognized the same stages and applied to them a variety of nomenclature. The three words used above, concentration, deliberation, and contemplation, have merely been selected by the writer as appropriate, and are not necessarily in line with the terms used by such authorities as Evelyn Underhill or Baron von Hügel. The sequence of experience is the important fact, namely, that there are three *stages* leading on to a fourth *state*.

4. *These three stages taken sequentially on one object are called samyāma.*
5. *Samyāma results in lucid knowledge.*
6. *It is progressive and can be applied at various levels.*
7. *Samyāma is the first step in true yoga, the five preliminary exercises merely leading up to this.*
8. *But samyāma is still not the goal.* (See I. 19.)

COMMENT. The practice of samyāma is one by which the mind becomes tuned in to the object of study, so that insight into it is developed and a wide range of correlated ideas become available.

The person who develops the faculty of samyāma has a creative understanding of anything to which he applies this faculty. Many apparently supernormal powers are due merely to a deeper interior knowledge such as may be obtained by the practice of samyāma.

The third stage has its dangers, since it can result in passive trance, which is a state of auto-hypnosis and is entirely unproductive.

The next four sutras analyse the development of mental control from another angle.

9. *When control of mind is achieved in the face of distraction, then the mind takes on a one-pointed form, which is itself a modification or trend in the mind.*

10. *By habitual practice the point of balance at which such one-pointedness dominates can be sustained at will.*

11. *The mind has two inherent tendencies, to consider many things and to become one-pointed. The quality of sustained one-pointedness leads to samādhi.*

12. *Then, by further achievement of balance between inertia and activity in the mind itself, a point is finally reached where all mental processes are transcended.*

COMMENT. The remainder of Book III deals chiefly with the use of samyāma in obtaining special knowledge, and explanations of its technique.

13. *Since matter, space, and time are the basic requisites of manifestation, it follows that any factor in the manifested universe may be taken as known when at a given moment its substance, form, and rate of change are cognized.*

COMMENT. This triplicity—matter, space, and time—refers again to the gunas. In the original Sanskrit version these gunas are subtly referred to in the three previous sutras, but in a manner that is practically untranslatable.

14-15. *All things exist potentially in prakriti, but can be manifested only through the infinitely varied interweaving of the three gunas.*

Sutras 16–49.

COMMENT. Since, as has been said in sutra 13, any factor in the manifested universe may be taken as known when its three qualities are fully cognized, it follows that if it is possible to gain this cognition in respect of any object or idea complete comprehension and mastery follow. The object then becomes the subject to the mind of the yogi. As the mind itself is a manifestation of the three gunas, the yogi can obtain mastery over the gunas by the discipline of the mind in samyāma. This leads on naturally to the control of other manifestations of the gunas external to the personal consciousness of the yogi, and ultimately to the control of all natural forces. This is the technical explanation of the occult or mysterious powers of the yogi called siddhis, such as control of pulse, heart-beat, etc., telepathy, levitation, supernormal physical strength, and the direction of physical forces at a distance (tele-kinesis).

Sutras 16 to 49 for the most part enumerate the objects upon which samyāma should be made in order to develop special powers. There seems no particular point to be gained by enumerating these in full.

Sutras 50–6.

COMMENT. The student is frequently reminded throughout these sutras that the siddhis or occult powers are a definite hindrance to unconscious samādhi or liberation (kaivalya). The concluding five or six sutras deal with the results of renunciation of interest in these powers, and the development of illumined discrimination through a right understanding of the relation between the spirit itself (purusha) and the balanced life (sattva) of the individual. Such discriminative knowledge discerns the difference even between apparently similar objects, transcends time and space, and is omniscient. When this is attained without attachment to any other state or power kaivalya or liberation is achieved.

BOOK IV

THE SEER AND THE SEEN

This fourth and final book is more purely metaphysical than the other three, and is largely concerned with a problem about which a vast amount has been thought and written in the west, namely the relation of mind to spirit. It expounds from the eastern point of view the arguments for the existence of a self or soul which is behind the mind and directs it. It is by the conscious realization of the true relation between the three factors, purusha or spirit, mind, and external phenomena, that the yogi attains his goal of kaivalya or liberation, and hence it is fitting that the exposition of yoga should end with a discussion of this relation.

Because this book is very abstruse in its substance, and because in detail it is not germane to the subject under discussion, it has been thought better in some cases to summarize the general drift of several sutras rather than to attempt a detailed rendering of each one.

The point that needs to be stressed as of particular significance to the general subject under discussion is that in the science of yoga the analysis of mental and emotional automatism is regarded as merely a preliminary exercise leading on to the discovery of the real nature of spiritual consciousness, i.e. of purusha. That this discovery is not an inevitable result of the overcoming of the obstacles is admitted, just as it is recognized that 'complete' analysis does not necessarily result in self-direction. The east suggests that further use and application of methods previously described, such as more complete detachment and deeper insight into the laws of nature, will ultimately bring about a direct experience of spirit (purusha) as the basic factor in human consciousness.

1. *A man may possess the siddhis as a gift from birth, or through taking certain drugs, or by reciting incantations, or by practising certain physical austerities, or as the result of samādhi.*

2. *The changes thus brought about in a man's body and soul are due to natural processes set up by these causes.*

3. *Good deeds are not the direct cause of this change, but they prepare the way for it by removing obstacles, just as evil deeds obstruct the change by creating obstacles.*

COMMENT. This sutra can also be rendered as follows: 'The apparent immediate cause is not the true cause of the siddhis. External behaviour merely removes obstacles.'

4. *One who has mastered the siddhis has the power of manifesting in various bodies simultaneously.*

5. *But these bodies are all under the control of his own mind.*

6. *When the siddhis are mastered by the practice of samādhi, then that which results from the siddhis does not create fresh karma.*

COMMENT. In sutra 1 the siddhis are said to be attained in five different ways, but sutra 6 indicates that only the last method, that of samādhi, is safe for the man who desires to be free from rebirth. For if occult powers are obtained by drugs, ascetic practices and the like, the soul is not really free, and in that case the powers may result in binding him more closely to the necessity for rebirth.

Sutras 7–16 deal with the law of cause and effect.

7–8. *Although the yogi, by detachment, has transcended*

the law of cause and effect (karma) in relation to
his actions, in the case of the ordinary man all
thoughts and deeds bring about results in due course.

9. *The effect of any action may be in abeyance for an in-*
definite period of time, but when suitable circumstances
arise it will become manifest.

COMMENT. The meaning of the sutra is that although no cause can be without effect, suitable and
congruous circumstances must arise before the
effect can be felt. The analyst sees this truth daily
in his practice, for the effect of childish happenings
may be latent for many years, and then, owing to
relevant circumstances, may suddenly become active. To the Hindu the sutra conveys the idea that
karma, be it pleasurable or painful, incurred in any
one life will not be fulfilled until an incarnation
occurs suitable for its fruition.

10. *The law of cause and effect is inherent in mind, and*
is coexistent with mind.

11. *The yogi who has attained liberation (kaivalya) is*
no longer in bondage to mental limitations (ignorance)
and hence is able to transcend this law.

12–16. *Yet the law of cause and effect and the world of*
phenomena in general do exist independently of the con-
sciousness of the yogi.

COMMENT. These sutras summarized above have
for their purpose the negation of the idea which
prevails in certain schools of eastern as of western

philosophy that the world of phenomena has no real existence except in the mind of the thinker.

Sutras 17–26 deal with the relationship of the seer to the mind.

17. *In order to know an object it is necessary for the mind to be able to reproduce that object in mental matter.*

18. *The seer (purusha) is constant and not subject to modifications and is therefore able to observe the modifications of the mind.*

COMMENT. Sutras 19, 20, 21 adduce various proofs of the existence of the seer apart from the mind.

19. *It is possible for the seer to know or cognize the mind as a thing apart.*

20. *The seer is necessary, since the mind cannot be aware of itself as an object.*

21. *The theory of multiplicity of minds cognizing each other would result in confusion.*

22. *The identification of the consciousness with the self or seer brings awareness of the mind as an object.*

23. *The mind reacts both to the seer and to the seen.*

COMMENT. The western world is familiar with the idea of mental processes being stimulated by external objects; the east adds to this the conception that the mind is also capable of reacting to the impulses of the spirit, or purusha, the seer. From the Hindu point of view there is no real knowledge without this twofold process.

24. *Though the mind has its automatic reactions, directed thinking is the result of its association with purusha.*

25. *Desire for knowledge as to the nature of the self is extinguished when the distinction between the self and the mind has been experienced.*

26. *Then the mind turns from attachment to the external world and is bent toward liberation (kaivalya).*

COMMENT. Sutras 27–34 deal with samādhi and kaivalya and the cessation of bondage to the gunas.

27. *The state of kaivalya is necessarily intermittent at first as distractions recur.*

28. *But these can be overcome by the methods already indicated.*

29. *If to full discriminative knowledge is added supreme non-attachment, then the yogi achieves a state called the 'cloud of virtue' which is the true spiritual consciousness.*

30. *Then comes freedom from distraction, and the bondage of the gunas is transcended.*

31. *Then in consequence of the infinity of knowledge the knowable becomes small.*

32. *The work of the gunas is now fulfilled.*

COMMENT. It is here understood that the work of the gunas is finished *for the yogi.* (See p. 128, sutras 12–16.)

33. *Time and space are transcended by the seer.*

34. *When the qualities of nature (gunas), having fulfilled their object, are re-absorbed, consciousness abides in its own essence; this is kaivalya.*

COMMENT. The following is a commentary expressed in Hindu phraseology which conveys the eastern sense of sublime fulfilment indicated in this closing sutra :

'Nature's task is done, this unselfish task which our sweet nurse Nature had imposed upon herself. As it were, she gently took the Self-forgetting soul by the hand, and showed him all the experiences in the universe, all manifestations, bringing him higher and higher through various bodies, till his glory came back, and he remembered his own nature. Then the kind mother went back the same way she came, for others who also have lost their way in the trackless desert of life. And thus is she working, without beginning and without end. And thus through pleasure and pain, through good and evil, the infinite river of souls is flowing into the ocean of perfection, of self-realization.

Glory unto those who have realized their own nature; may their blessings be on us all.'[1]

[1] *Raja Yoga*, by Vivekananda, publ. Kegan Paul.

PART III

A COMPARISON

Chapter VIII

MODIFICATIONS OF THE THINKING PRINCIPLE: CONFUSED THOUGHT

SINCE our object is to examine into possible resemblances between analytical therapy and yoga and not to write a treatise on the yoga sutras, I propose to select from the vast mass of material wrapped up in the aphorisms as set forth in the preceding chapter a few outstanding points for comparison with western psychological ideas. Whenever possible, reference will be made to specific sutras or groups of sutras.

In the present chapter I propose to examine the sutras which describe the mento-emotional state of the ordinary man.[1]

In his ordinary state, says Patanjali, man is not self-aware, but is lost in his own confused picture of life. He has three possible ways of gaining right knowledge of the phenomenal world, namely by direct observation, by the use of reliable information, and by inference from either of these two sources. But in actual fact his direct observation is faulty, his sources of information are unreliable, and

[1] Book I, sutras 2–11, 20, 21, 30, 31.

his inferences inaccurate. Hence his mind is usually occupied in confused thinking or in fancy, and his own past experience (i.e. memory) is not to be relied on. The habit of confused thinking may be overcome by determined one-pointed effort to recover accurate memory of past experience and to acquire discrimination.[1]

Many are desirous of acquiring these gifts but are hindered by ill health, or become bored and lack energy to persist, or are by nature incapable of perceiving what is required of them. People who desire to clarify their mental confusion but are unable to overcome difficulties become depressed or are subject to other nervous disorders.[2]

The above represents approximately what Patanjali has to say about the state of mind of the ordinary man who is immersed in life at the mento-emotional level and whose thought is mainly concrete and repetitive. Few people realize how repetitive and hence automatic the vast majority of everyday thinking is. Every morning we have to 'think' what clothes we will put on, and what breakfast we will eat; but our thoughts on these subjects are likely to follow one of two or three well-worn tracks. Clothes—cold—flannels—overcoat; or, clothes—wet—thick boots—mackintosh; breakfast—hungry—eggs and bacon—toast and

[1] I. 4, 7, 20. [2] I. 30, 31.

marmalade; or, breakfast—headache—dry toast—
tea, &c. And so throughout the day follow hundreds
of decisions based on *habits* of thought, and not on
any immediate consideration of facts. For example,
a heavy breakfast is an automatic response to feeling
fit and hungry, but if one is going immediately after
breakfast to do some hard mental work or even to
play vigorous tennis it might have been better to
reconsider the breakfast question before eating it.
Most of us reconsider it, fruitlessly, when it is too
late!

This automatism of thought extends far beyond
the everyday needs of the body. The whole of
human life at its present stage is confused and
shadowed by a mass of so-called thought which
is the outcome of false observation, unreliable information, and faulty inference. This fact most
serious-minded people of our own day realize pretty
fully. Let us consider what has given rise to it.

In the long evolutionary history of man, his body,
his emotions and his mind have been successively
trained, with great effort, to a certain state of
efficiency, to a certain degree of perfection. There
was a time when the gradual development of an
adequate and hence relatively perfect physical
body was the most serious work of the race. At
that epoch the development of the body was man's
legitimate goal, and he had, as it were, a right

to be absorbed in the physical world. At a later stage came the unfolding of the emotions and the concrete mind. In a sense emotion and mind developed simultaneously, but in another sense the emotional growth preceded the mental. It is generally accepted that a young child recapitulates in a short time the evolutionary stages of the race, first bringing its physical body to a certain degree of efficiency, and then beginning consciously to exercise its emotions of love, hatred, attraction, repulsion, anger, jealousy, &c., before it can deliberately reason. All through the childhood years it is normal that the emotional nature should be more developed than the mentality.[1] We accept the fact that a child can experience extremes of joy and sorrow long before it can do much in the way of thought or reasoning, but we accept it without considering the importance of that fact in human evolution. At the present day many novels are written describing the emotional joys and still more the despairs of childhood. They are depicted as being of very great intensity, dramatic, poignant, heart-breaking; and to the adult observer part of their tragedy lies in the fact that they are often about trivial things, the lost kitten, the broken doll, all alone in the dark, no one to play with, mother

[1] i.e. normal for the average person. A very fair percentage of exceptions always exist, and especially so to-day.

gone away for a visit. Why is it that so large a proportion of childhood's sorrows and joys make the
adult smile? Is it not just because the emotional
capacity of a child is wellnigh full-grown while its
mentality is still embryonic and incapable of seeing
things in proportion?

During the first few years of life, that period
which educationists have always recognized as so
important, the child feels greatly, and thinks very
little. Consider this in relation to the time-worn
saying of the Jesuits—'Give us the first seven years
of a child's life, and the rest is immaterial!' We
have always understood this to mean that these are
par excellence the *habit-forming* years. Then what are
habits? Certainly they are not the outcome of
thought, nor are they merely physical automatisms.
The view of the modern psychologist is that they
are to a large extent crystallized emotion, and result mainly from more or less skilful manipulation
by the adult of the child's fear of punishment and
love of approbation. An infant learns control of
its bodily functions not in the ordinary course of
nature nor through its own preference for cleanli-
ness, but through a desire to win its mother's or
nurse's approbation or to escape punishment.
Young children are by nature wholly indifferent to
dirt in all forms, have no sense of shame in regard to
their bodily functions, love noise, and enjoy destroy·

ing property. All these natural tendencies we have felt obliged for various reasons to suppress and to replace by standards of our own, and this is usually achieved by playing on fear and love of approbation. Hence almost the entire early training of a child necessarily consists in the imposition of standards through an emotional appeal.

A little later such habits as truthfulness and respect for other people's property are inculcated in exactly the same way, with the possible addition of the powerful factor of God and religion. If a child refrains from lying and stealing and so forms habits of truthfulness and honesty, it is largely because he is afraid or ashamed of doing otherwise, i.e. afraid of punishment or ashamed of disapprobation, not because he has brought his reason to bear on the question.

Little by little the whole skeleton or framework of his life is built up on this system, and he acquires a set of 'opinions' and 'standards' based on his fear of acting contrary to the accepted habits of his environment, and having for him a very deep emotional value, but not a great deal of thought-value. It is of course true that the reaction to environmental pressure is by no means always submissive, for there are a number of children in whom this parental compulsion produces an opposite reaction, and enhances to an extreme degree the love of dirt, noise, destructiveness, and all the anti-social tendencies. These are the little rebels who in a poorer environment become child-delinquents, while in well-to-do homes they merely destroy the family peace. Their rebellion is obviously not the result of considered thought, but another form of emotional automatism.

The psychology of conscience is an aspect of the subject that has been deeply studied by the various schools of psychotherapy. The Freudian regards conscience as a compulsive automatism, the result of the child's early identification of himself with his parents and their standards. He considers that man's higher nature and idealistic promptings are an outcome of what he calls the super-ego, and that these promptings come in childhood from the unconscious and are a source of conflict and neurosis until they become self-conscious. Thus a man's horror of card-playing or smoking is likely to be an automatic survival of parental standards of morality. The idea rouses him to emotional outbursts and an effort to enforce his opinions on the community. As an alternative it is of course possible that he has consciously thought the matter out, and has decided that smoking injures the nervous system, or that card-playing is undesirable for himself because he has a strong love of gambling.

Adler's view of compulsive behaviour differs

somewhat from Freud's. He considers it to be due not to fixation on the parent but to some congenital handicap or inferiority, for which the child tries to compensate by arranging a style of life which is an automatic and not a conscious mechanism for overcoming his difficulty.

When childhood is past and adolescence sets in the capacity for thought gradually develops, and the youth begins to think out his personal problems. But it is only the rare spirit who at this stage questions his own opinion-habits and standard-habits. These are already fixed, and he builds his thoughts *on them*. He begins to discriminate, but his choices are only in appearance based on reason. For example, if he is an average public schoolboy he regards his home and school standards of ethics and conduct as axiomatic, as something to argue from, not something to argue about. As some one has said, the child covers the slate of consciousness with very large writing, and the adult writes smaller and then smaller over the child's writing and in the interstices.

It is not easy to generalize about the way in which people think from adolescence onward, because an increasing divergence of type then becomes an important factor. One very large group or class may be said practically never to indulge in thought at all. They are content to fit into the framework of

their birth and environment entirely without question. Another group, a very numerous one at the
present day, begins questioning as soon as early
childhood is past, and still another goes on accepting with a certain undercurrent of question and
misgiving, until in the thirties and forties they begin
to awake to a realization that they are profoundly
dissatisfied with life and have no idea why. At
whatever period the onset of questioning may occur
it always, as every one is aware, brings with it fierce
conflict, unrest, struggle, often profound misery.
The struggle is, in essence, the effort to disentangle
truth and reality from the impenetrable thicket of
habit conditioned by emotion in which it has become entangled. It is a crucial one in man's evolution, and as a rule he attacks it without any conception at all of its immensity. He is like Asa Thor
trying to drain the cup of penance, unaware that
he is in reality attempting to drink up the ocean.

The difficulty of gaining a clear perception of any
human problem is the difficulty of seeing it impersonally, of freeing it from the habitual emotional
associations that surround it. Take a trivial case—
you are undecided as to whether you will pay a
necessary call on a wet afternoon. You are unable
to form an impartial judgement of the urgency of
the call versus the undesirability of getting wet,
because you are in a state of emotional conflict

between a sense of 'oughtness' and a dislike of turning out in the damp; i.e. a fear of self-disapprobation is in conflict with a fear of discomfort. While you make all sorts of apparently reasonable remarks as to why you should or should not go, these two alternate in the consciousness to the exclusion of any real consideration of the objective facts of the case. To take other examples—exactly why do you want your son to go to Harrow? Exactly why do you approve or disapprove of Mussolini, of home rule for India, of the Soviet Government in Russia, of the Labour party, of the Conservative party, of fox-hunting, of the Anglo-Catholics, of the Spiritualists? How much of your opinion is based on family tradition, on fear of or desire for change, on class-prejudice, on fear of want and poverty, on fear of personal loss, on fear of seeming to be a crank? If your opinions were *entirely* based on emotion, on personal like and dislike, without any particular objective facts to support them, your problem would be far easier. It is the intricate confusion of fact and emotion, it is the skill with which personal desire presents to you perfectly good and adequate reasons for your cherished opinions, that make the conflict so acute and real candour so rare and so difficult.

As has been said, to a great many people the time comes when the attainment of a candid outlook on life, of a freedom from mental and emotional confusion, of actual contact with reality, becomes crucial. The necessity may arise from ill health, from unhappiness, or from sheer spiritual hunger and thirst; but whatever the cause the result is the same—they become conscious that there is a pearl of great price, to purchase which everything they possess must be sold.

One recalls the story of Prince Gotama, whether historical or not is immaterial, for it is of the most profound symbolic truth. The young prince, representing in a sense Everyman, is deliberately supplied by his parents with a complete world of fantasy, in which he lives outwardly happy but inwardly uneasy until he has attained manhood. At last he insists upon leaving his enchanted garden and takes an experimental journey into the outer world. The king and queen do all they can to make the outer world appear consistent with the fantasy world they have created for their beloved son, but in spite of them he catches disturbing glimpses of reality, and from that moment his soul knows no rest until it has faced stark facts and made a real and profound adaptation to them. It takes him a lifetime of struggle, and he is deceived again and again into accepting traditional means of evasion —but in the end he attains illumination. This is up to a point a parable of the experience of a large part of the human race, one might perhaps say of the whole of civilized humanity. Parents and social tradition construct round us in childhood a world of fantasy; and the majority of us at adolescence make an abortive attempt to break away but return perforce for a time. Many are content thereafter to spend their lives in the fantasy world because it appears pleasanter; others get to the stage of mistrusting the unreality and restlessly desiring to break through, but find themselves unwilling to face the tremendous cost; a few, like Prince Gotama, are resolute enough to hew their way out.

In all ages of world history methods have been devised by the more enlightened for the help and guidance of the determined seeker after reality, and in comparing yoga and analytical therapy I am attempting to make a useful contact between one of the most ancient and one of the most modern of these. I should like to show that on the one hand the yoga sutras of Patanjali are not merely an archaic curiosity, and that on the other hand analytical therapy is not a wholly new discovery, but is in harmony with the wisdom of an ancient civilization famed for its insight and its profound philosophies.

Let us return to a consideration of the extent to which there can be found in the sutras ideas similar to our western ones about mento-emotional automatism or confused thinking.

At the beginning of his treatise Patanjali states that the activities of the mind include correct understanding, misconception, fancy, sleep (i.e. dream), and remembrance. In other words, the mind can by accurate observation or inference gain a correct idea, or by inaccurate observation and wrong inference it can gain a false one. It can be lost in a maze of verbal delusion unrelated to reality, it can recollect impressions of past experience, and it has a sleep-activity when the physical senses are in abeyance.[1]

All these five activities are constantly at work in the mind of the ordinary man, but he has no real mastery over them. In the course of a day he may experience instances of correct apprehension—it is five o'clock, the telephone bell is ringing, a north wind is blowing; and of incorrect apprehension if the clock happens to be wrong, or if he has a strong desire or fear connected with the hour of five which may cause him to miscount the stroke. He may carry on a discussion of which he has misunderstood the premises; he may deliberately recall a business interview of last week; or he may take an after-dinner nap and dream strange dreams. But of all these processes he has only partial control; he cannot ensure for himself correct apprehension, nor can he always recall a given set of facts at will; he is

[1] I. 6–9, 11.

often misled by his own fanciful delusions, and when he falls asleep he may be the unwilling victim of nightmare.

Now the analyst assures us that the greater part of our mistakes about facts, our false reasonings, our independable memories, our nagging and unwelcome anxiety-states, and above all our sleeping and waking nightmares, are due to mento-emotional conflict, conflict between actual fact and our own desires and fears. If, says the analyst, we can resolve these conflicts and disentangle the fact itself from our emotion about the fact, we shall be free and masters of ourselves.

Patanjali says that the activity of the thinking principle can be controlled by steady practice and by non-attachment or dispassion, and he explains non-attachment as being 'that effect which comes to those who have given up their thirst after objects'.[1] By non-attachment he does not mean compulsive sense of duty, a turning away from the desired object, leaving it active though repressed; but a loosening of the tensions of the psyche, and in particular a non-identification of one's self with experience.[2] He goes on to say that people fail to attain any degree of detachment and dispassion because to do so steady and unremitting effort is

[1] I. 12, 15 (Vivekananda's version).
[2] II. 17, 18, 20, 21; and also latter part of introductory remarks on p. 110.

necessary, and this is difficult because of such obstacles as ill health, absorption in small anxieties of daily life or worldly ambitions, irresolution, laziness, self-indulgence, lack of intelligent understanding of the method to be pursued or doubt of its efficacy. When any one has so far progressed as to be conscious of his need for mental discipline, has tried to achieve it and has failed because of one or other of the above obstacles, he is likely to be beset by depression, nervous unrest, and a general disturbance of function. To overcome these initial difficulties the attention should be directed toward some absorbing and impersonal idea, i.e. some form of deliberate meditation must be practised.[1]

All this bears a very clear relation to the experience and method of the analyst. A large number of the patients who come to him are deeply self-dissatisfied, but have neither the energy, the confidence, nor the skill to help themselves. They are constantly in ill health, tortured by petty worries or social ambitions, irresolute, nerve-ridden and depressed. In short, the picture that Patanjali gives of the state of mind of the aspirant toward yoga is almost point for point a description of the typical patient who seeks analytical therapy because his disease of mind or body has become intolerable to him.

[1] I. 30, 31, 32.

The analyst holds that a person in this state of ill health, irresolution and general instability is practically incapable of self-help. The eastern student is so early accustomed to the idea of meditation that to him it seems possible to undertake for one's self a discipline which will bring about liberation; but even he admits that success comes to few unless they can find a teacher or guru who will train them.

While the analyst rarely counsels actual meditation, many schools of analysis advocate the practice of inducing a patient to steady his nerves and combat his depression by taking up some absorbing occupation such as painting or a craft, which to some small extent resembles in effect what Patanjali calls 'intense application to any one thing'. The long duration of some analyses and on the other hand the failure of some apparently analysed patients to be able to take a constructive attitude may be due to the fact that the need for some form of directed or active therapy has been overlooked or ignored by the analyst at a critical moment.

It would appear then that there is a fair basis for comparison between what the yogi calls a state of confused perception and the mental and emotional condition with which the analyst commonly has to deal.

Chapter IX
MODIFICATIONS OF THE THINKING PRINCIPLE: CLEAR THINKING

THE most practically significant of the four books of the yoga sutras for the western reader or student is the second, since it contains preliminary instructions for those who have not had any yoga training, whereas Books III and IV deal mainly with advanced stages of the science. In other words Book II takes up the question at about the point where the psychotherapist also meets it, the point where dissatisfaction with what we have called confused thinking drives the person to a serious consideration of what can be done to remedy it.

The view of both yogi and analyst is that nothing can be done unless the person is willing to alter the entire habit of his mind and emotions from the ground up. This is a large task, and Patanjali begins by stating that the candidate for yoga at this stage finds a threefold attitude of mind necessary. He requires discipline or relaxation of tension, study or aspiration, and resignation to God. This sutra might also read that he requires self-discipline, study of suitable material, and an attitude of acceptance towards life.[1]

[1] II. 1.

At first sight the inevitability of these requisites is not obvious, but further consideration throws light on the matter.

The word which we have rendered by discipline is commonly translated as mortification, and has primary reference to fasts and other bodily penances. The admitted purpose of bodily austerities is to break the fixity and automatism of habit at the physical level, and to make the body more amenable to the dictates of the will. The idea of mortification as used here is probably a much wider one. To 'mortify the flesh' is to treat the body in such a way as to overcome its demands, to induce a relaxation of the grip of bodily desires, so that mind and spirit are no longer hampered by them. Preliminary yoga demands a much more extensive loosening of grip or tension than this, a relaxation not only of physical habits but of mental and emotional automatisms; and this latter is a far subtler and more difficult achievement. People are brought up to recognize that it is undesirable to be dominated by the needs and habits of the body, but they are on the whole somewhat pleased with their habits of thought and feeling, which they pride themselves upon as matters of family or racial tradition or as rather interesting personal idiosyncrasies. This point has been dealt with in the preceding chapter, but it is worth repeating here that the man who is

seriously endeavouring to extricate himself from
his mento-emotional automatisms must face the
necessity of relaxing his hold on what seems to him
to be all that is valuable in life. There is scarcely an
object or an idea in his whole universe but needs a
fresh evaluation. Nothing is as he thought it was.
Every absolute on which he has based his life becomes once more relative. He may find that he has
not a single moral or social standard left on which
to pin his trust. He may even realize with a kind of
impotent rage that the things he has most admired
and respected are trivial, and yet from sheer emotional habit he goes on admiring them. Things he
has despised and shrunk from are seen to be of in-
estimable worth, and yet he continues to be repelled
by them. His snap judgements on events of the day,
his habitual method of summing up the actions and
ideas of his fellow-men have to go, and he must
needs study each on its own merits. It is, moreover,
not only other people and things that need to be
looked at afresh. Of his world of confused fantasy
he himself has always been a part, and the most
difficult and searching portion of his task is to see
his own personality stark, unveiled by illusion.
Such a relinquishment of fixed mento-emotional
habit and the attainment of a new set of values is a
result of clear thinking, but it is also a preliminary
necessity for clear thinking, so that there is a phase

when the student is in the awkward position of the would-be swimmer who cannot really learn to swim unless he is in deep water, and yet cannot support himself with any comfort and security in deep water until he has mastered the art of swimming. The standards, judgements and rules of conduct on which a person has been brought up, the objects which he has been taught to think are worth living for and fighting for, these are his moral and emotional terra firma, and to relinquish them without having first acquired others is indeed to strike out from the shore without knowing whether he will sink or float. Yet obviously it is not possible to acquire the capacity for clear thinking unless one is willing to relinquish the comfortable accustomed fruits of confused thinking.

It is an interesting fact and one of very wide validity that any real step forward in life has to be not so much a step as a leap in the dark, with a dreaded moment of uncertainty in mid-air. The stepping-stones are rarely close enough together to permit of secure progression.

There is still another sense in which relaxation of tension is a necessary preliminary to yoga. The ordinary state of consciousness in which people live is one of more or less acute psychological tension, for most of us spend our lives in efforts to get what we consider necessary and desirable and to avoid what we consider harmful and unpleasant. Very tense effort, accompanied by a deep though often unconscious sense of compulsion, may be directed toward maintaining social prestige, achieving fame, living a strictly religious life, acquiring wealth and a comfortable standard of living, writing a learned book, succeeding in one's profession, becoming a good golfer, bringing up one's children adequately—with a corresponding struggle to avoid all the pitfalls that may prevent the attainment of these goals. We need to admit freely that such a compulsive attitude toward life is stimulating to the human being up to a certain stage in his development, but the candidate for yoga should have reached the point where he is willing to relax the tense grip of fear and desire which forces activity upon him whether he wills it or not.

The second requisite, study or aspiration, is a more obvious one. Thought, enthusiasm, a shaping of the mind, a deletion of other objects and a concentrating on the one object with fervency, are necessary for any great undertaking. The word study should not be taken in the sense of collecting information, or acquiring knowledge from books, but rather of tuning in the whole nature to a given wave-length, of letting the mind become absorbed in the subject in hand. In the ordinary projects and enterprises of life we take this requisite of study for granted. The man who is deeply ambitious of success in a career instinctively devotes himself heart and soul, day and night, to that aim, and subordinates all else to it. He sacrifices leisure, luxury and personal pleasure, and sees all the events of life as either furthering or hindering his schemes. In some translations this second requisite is rendered as 'muttering', to the bewilderment of the western reader. The yogi does actually devote himself to his object by spending hours daily in muttering or repeating to himself the sacred mantras or versicles which his guru prescribes for him. These mantras are ancient formulas, so devised as to be effective not only in meaning but also in sound, and when recited with the correct and traditional intonation are said to assist in detaching the consciousness from the preoccupation of ordinary existence and clarifying and stilling the mind.

The third requisite is resignation to the will of God or Ishvara. Some commentators read this phrase as describing the relation of the disciple to his guru or teacher. In the east this is always one of absolute submission to the will of the elder. Apart from the necessity for acceptance of and submission to the teacher there is also involved in this third requirement the need for a profound acceptance of the conditions of individual life. Attitudes of mind such as ambition, resentment, discontent in face of the inevitable, rebellion, are recognized as anti-pathetic to the mastery of the mind and emotions. The ambitious or resentful person is never sufficiently at leisure from himself to achieve the recollectedness and concentration of faculty necessary for the practice of yoga.

There is, however, a much subtler and more elusive reason why acceptance is one of the fundamental necessities. For all the loftier achievements of living an unimpeded flow of life-force or libido or spiritual energy is necessary. It is possible to exist automatically with the life-force dammed back, but creative awareness demands a free flow. The creative act, at whatever level, is a fourfold experience in which the urge to express or the aspiration to achieve is followed by a blending of the self with the material to be used or the object of aspiration. Upon this there follows a period of effort or struggle, and the climax or achievement of the goal brings ecstasy and peace. There is a sense in which yoga is the supreme creative activity, and the feeling of wholeness, oneness, freedom, of having all one's faculties in alignment and harmony, of being afloat upon the stream of being and void of resentment or shrinking, is a necessary preliminary to the more advanced yoga practices. This experience of union with life, which the translators have called 'resignation to Ishvara' is not possible where there is non-acceptance of life's conditions, a resentful wish to be otherwise or to have otherwise, or a critical attitude to things and to people as they are. Certain discontents are said to be divine, because they lead to creative activity. The man who is sufficiently discontented with his environment is likely in course of time to create a new environment, while the man who is sufficiently discontented with himself is likely to create a new self. The student of yoga has need to be so intent on the creation of a new self that he has no leisure for grumbling at his environment.

If it is the case that preliminary yoga is a process akin to analytical therapy, these three requisites for yoga ought to be in some sense familiar to the analyst in relation to his patients, and I think it will be generally admitted that they are so. Let us consider them in a different order from that in which they are enumerated in the sutra, and look at study or aspiration first. We have seen that there are two types of analysand with which every analyst is familiar, the person who seeks relief from an urgent and disabling condition of mind and body and is satisfied when such relief is obtained, and the person who is seriously demanding self-knowledge and re-orientation. It is obvious that the former type has no very close kinship with the student of yoga, and can accordingly be dismissed from this discussion.

The person who is desirous of a deep analysis is obliged to embark on the project at least as whole-heartedly as he would embark on an exploring expedition in the physical world, and must be prepared to make large sacrifices of time money and energy, devoting himself one-pointedly to the end in view. His mind must be turned to it with deepest attention, and he has need to be an alert and active participator in the mento-emotional exploration he is undertaking. Not everyone realizes this, or realizing it is prepared to accept it as a condition of speedy success; for, as Patanjali truly says, some would-be students are but dabblers, some are serious in their efforts, but only the few are entirely one-pointed.[1]

No sooner does actual analysis begin than the patient becomes at once aware of a need for loosening of tension at all levels such as he has probably never dreamt of before. As a rule he is told to take up some position of physical relaxation which may or may not be fairly easy of achievement. He is then asked to relax his hold upon his mind in such a way as will permit his every passing thought and sensation to register and to be expressed aloud in words. This game of free association requires effort, skill, and complete sincerity of intention, and few are able to play it without a good deal of practice. To

[1] I. 22.

let go by an effort of will the habit of verbal continence which has been built up from babyhood, and
is fortified by all our subtlest feelings of self-esteem
shame and embarrassment, is in every sense of the
word an exercise in mortification and relaxation
of tension.

A deeper and more far-reaching type of relaxation has to be achieved in the later stages, for as in
yoga so also in analysis confused habits of thought
based on childish emotions and on traditional reactions have to be broken up in order to make clear
thinking possible. A large part of the work of the
analyst consists in helping the patient to release his
tense hold on fixed ideas of personal inferiority, of
sin and guilt, of fear, of self-importance, and the
like. All that has been said in the preceding pages
with regard to the yogi's need for an entire readjustment of outlook and restatement of values applies
equally to the person who is undergoing analysis.
He also usually passes through a period of insecurity
when the old has failed him and the new is too unfamiliar to be at all comfortable, and the peculiar
sensation of relief when some cherished fantasy
about himself or his environment breaks off from
his mind and floats away into limbo is one of the
characteristic and valid analytical experiences.

The third requisite for yoga, 'resignation to Ishvara' or acceptance, is in a sense comparable to the

preliminary stage of what the analyst calls sublimation, the goal of analytical therapy. To accept life as it comes, to accept people as they are, to accept one's own inherent limitations and deal with them on a reality basis rather than by fantasy, are all part of the task of sublimation. It is by non-acceptance of reality that the life-force or libido is dammed, so that creative activity becomes impossible. The deeper forms of analysis aim at freeing libido and enabling the individual to unite with life, and by so doing to attain his own maximum development.

Chapter X

THE FIVE OBSTACLES

HAVING stated and defined the three necessary preliminary qualifications for yoga, Patanjali proceeds to deal with certain specific hindrances or obstacles which will be met with in its pursuit. He enumerates the five major hindrances as follows: ignorance, self-esteem, desire, aversion, and the will to live or attachment to life. I propose, as usual, to discuss these five obstacles first from the standpoint of yoga, and then to consider to what extent they are basic in analytical therapy.

Ignorance, says Patanjali, is the primary obstacle, and is the cause or root of the other four. The eastern idea of ignorance may be compared with the Christian conception of original sin. Just as the Christian is said to be 'born in sin' and to have as his object in life a battle with sin, so in the east the individual is regarded as being born into ignorance, as existing in a world of illusion built up by ignorance. The goal of evolution is the dispelling of ignorance, as the goal of a Christian life is the conquest of sin. When ignorance is completely dispelled, the man attains liberation, i.e. freedom from the bondage of reincarnation and compulsory experience; when sin is vanquished the Christian attains heaven.

Ignorance is the cause of all sorrow and suffering, because it is the cause of all conditioned experience.

Self-esteem, egoism, the sense of the supreme importance of the 'I', is a universal result of ignorance. The need of the self to expand, to gain power, to make itself felt, is inherent in every man. No one is free from it, for it is the necessary urge that in the earlier stages of evolution drives him on to fresh effort; but it is an illusion, and as he approaches nearer to reality he must painfully discard it. The candidate for yoga is deliberately trying to hasten his own evolution toward reality, and for him self-esteem is a serious obstacle.

Desire is the illusion by which man is identified with, entangled in experience. The term covers the entire range of sensational and emotional experience. It includes the craving for food, activity, or rest, the love of comfort in which is involved the desire to escape discomfort, the craving for excitement and for amusement, the love of home and friends, the pleasure of possessing, the urge of sex, the ecstasy of the artist, the adoration of the devotee. An infinite elaboration of enticement draws the soul toward the experience through which it must pass, and man becomes so identified with his emotions that he is unable to realize himself as existing apart from them. It is part of the yoga training to 'kill out desire', but this familiar phrase does not mean a withdrawal from human experience, because experience is the valid means of growth. It is from the sense of identity with experience that the candidate must extricate himself. By continual practice he learns to realize that the cravings of the physical body, the constant play of the emotions, the automatic weaving and interweaving of the ever-active mind, are exterior to an inner consciousness which is himself. Experience then becomes more objective, less enthralling and yet in a sense more interesting. Instead of being used by it he uses it, and is the master where once he was the slave; he is the rider of his steed, not the passenger it carries. As such he can choose what he will think and also what he will feel. If he chooses to be angry anger comes, but his inner being is not shaken by it; if he chooses the experience of love he is the conscious lover and not the victim of an entangling passion. Moreover, he is no longer impelled to wallow in experience, to rest in a sense of pleasure until the pleasure is exhausted, to be shaken by grief until grief itself is a weariness.

The distinction between this technique and what is ordinarily known as repression is a real one; for whereas repression is the automatic unconscious refusal to permit an experience to come into the field of consciousness, the yoga technique involves the objectifying of experience and then the acceptance or rejection of it by reference to the conscious choice of the self. This habit of regulating the emotional life by a process of withdrawal and choice is very difficult to acquire, and a lifetime may be spent in learning the rudiments of it. Nevertheless, it is by no means entirely foreign to the western point of view, for in the smaller happenings of every day a great many people habitually attempt it. Thus, I am going out for the evening and find that some one has borrowed my latch-key and forgotten to return it. Either I become automatically irritated and lose my temper, or I am sufficiently recollected and aware to take note of the irritation that is rising in me, to reject it as a useless and tiring way of meeting the emergency, and to choose to go and find another key. In the former case I have identified myself with the situation, in the latter I have objectified it and by a reference to self have refused the useless emotion. It is quite common also to deal with the emotion of fear in this way. I can remember an amusing incident of my school-days which illustrates this point. It was the fashion among us to be hysterically terrified of a large and sticky insect which we called a June-bug, but which I believe is technically known as a cockchafer. On one hot summer night there were several of these monsters in the dormitory, and wild screams indicated that a fit of mass hysterics was imminent. I was

involved in the group fear of the insect, but feeling
obliged somehow to cope with the situation I said
to myself, 'Those sticky, noisy monsters are in reality
perfectly harmless; it is only a habit that makes us
shriek at them. I can easily catch them and put
them out and avoid a row.' In other words, a mere
child is capable of objectifying and then refusing or
accepting an emotion. Alice in Wonderland objectified an emotion and refused it when she said
'They're only a pack of cards'. If she had said 'This
is a court of law and these terrible people can be-
head me; I am terrified but I must be a brave girl',
she would have shown courage, but she would have
been identified with the emotional situation instead
of outside it, and would have been suppressing fear.
Similarly if I had said 'I am terrified of those June-
bugs, but it is my duty to deal with them', the exterior result might have been the same, but the
interior technique entirely different. If Alice continued to impose upon herself the ego ideal or exterior social standard of being 'a brave girl' in all
such situations, she would ultimately repress a large
amount of libido and develop fixed attitudes or
complexes in regard to similar occasions. The reference to self which Alice made, bringing in a real
standard of her own consciousness (They are only
a pack of cards), or which I made (That June-bug
is really harmless) is a mode of reaction which

eliminates needless or fantasied feeling. It is a reaction based on reality.

A much more difficult art, and one that comparatively few ever realize to be possible, is that of evoking by choice a given emotion. It is true that many people habitually work themselves up into a frenzy of this or that because they enjoy the excitement, but they do not do it consciously, and would greatly resent the idea that it was deliberate. It is commonly considered that all genuine emotion must be evoked by an external situation, and that a deliberate and self-chosen feeling is a sham. I have often wondered why this idea is so general, because as I will show presently it is by no means in accordance with our ordinary practice; and I believe it due to the fact that in civilized communities we are from babyhood compelled by public opinion to make a constant pretence of the emotions of love and affection. It is *de rigueur* to 'love' not only our brothers and sisters but also our uncles and aunts and cousins, a very considerable number of whom we probably dislike intensely. The 'love' that we dole out to these people at Christmas and on other suitable occasions is well known to us to be a shameful pretence. We dare not say so, but we feel it acutely, and hence we grow up with the idea that the only genuine love is that which is spontaneously evoked in us when we meet a person who attracts us. When it is suggested that we can be deliberate about our emotions we immediately hear a hortatory voice from childhood saying, 'But you must try to love your Cousin Mary, dear. Just think what a lovely book she gave you for your birthday.' Similarly and for all too similar reasons are we told that we must 'love' God, and we suffer from a really acute guilt-sense at having no idea how to do it; for though we may have rebellious doubts about the need for loving Cousin Mary, we perfectly see that we ought to love God—if we only could. For some such reason as this people are very sceptical of self-conscious choice in regard to emotion. Nevertheless such choice is perfectly possible. For instance, it will be admitted that enthusiasm is an emotion, and it will also be admitted that if one deliberately chooses to work up an enthusiasm for a given subject, and is willing to give to the process the necessary hard work and drudgery and persistence, a genuine and pleasurable response will in time be developed. In exactly the same way it is possible to produce any other emotion, not faked but genuine, if it is felt to be worth the very considerable trouble that it necessitates. This evoking of an emotion is often met with in married life. A woman who realizes that the man she has married is not the phantasied hero of her dreams will sometimes control the emotional situation by deliberately realizing and dwelling upon the lovable and admirable facets of his nature until there grows up a feeling of understanding and comradeship and sympathy that is a not ineffective substitute for spontaneous passion. It is this self-conscious mastery of the emotional nature that yoga demands, and its lack is the hindrance that Patanjali names 'desire'.

The third hindrance or obstacle is aversion or hate, and it is usually stated in the commentaries that this is merely the opposite of the previous one, desire. But it would seem to me that this is true only in part. Whereas desire, the entanglement of the self in experience, is predominantly a question of the emotions, and its true opposite is hate, aversion is an obstacle occasioned by the workings of the concrete mind. As has been said repeatedly, emotion and concrete mind are so intermingled that it is not possible to separate them from each other, but the predominance of one or the other is normal to consciousness, and in the case of the third obstacle mind is often the larger factor. The concrete mind is to a great extent occupied in noting differences and making critical comparisons. In his more primitive states man uses this faculty almost entirely to enable him to get the best for himself. He sharpens his wits by seeing which is the better of two objects and grabbing it. The more civilized man comes to use his critical faculty for its own sake, because it satisfies his self-esteem to discriminate and pass judgement, without any necessary reference to material gain. In time man discovers that the untrained critical faculty is almost entirely destructive, and is on the whole more harmful than useful to the community. Consequently he devises means of training the faculty to constructive uses, and the advanced work of university students is largely concerned with the development of the capacity to compare and to appraise.

The fact that the critical faculty used destructively is anti-social and separative and that it feeds self-esteem makes it a very definite barrier to training in yoga, the whole trend of which is toward the recognition of unity and brotherliness. Although the yogi and the mystic are following widely different paths, yet their ends are similar, and a study of the lives of the saints shows in how many cases their first step has consisted in breaking down the barrier of separation, of shrinking, of critical superiority. In a well-known autobiographical study, *A Wanderer's Way* by Canon Raven, the writer describes in some detail the steps that led to his own 'conversion' or mystical illumination.' He makes the plunge from the life of a brilliant and popular Cambridge graduate into that of an office clerk in Liverpool. His inefficiency as a clerk wounds his academic self-esteem; he is unhappy and lonely, and after the usual preliminary period of darkness and despair, he begins to find himself through experience gained at a boys' club.

'This new experiment, incompetent as I was at it, was pure joy. When once the first shyness had worn off, and we began to feel at home together, there was a happiness in the club nights of quite a new kind. . . . Fellowship of such a sort had not come my way, fellowship in which *one's brains and position, one's ambitions and fears, ceased to matter,* fellowship in which the welfare of the children came first, *and all the artificial distinctions of class and book-learning were done away.*

We were just a big family: I was one of the weakest of its members, but I was welcome and belonged to it, and in it could get away from externals to elementals.'[1]

The writer goes on to link this experience of breaking through the barriers of self-esteem and social and educational separativeness with his first clear and definite perception of spiritual reality, although the connexion existed wholly in his interior consciousness, for in time and place the mystical experience had no definable connexion with the Liverpool club.

In thus linking Patanjali's obstacle of 'aversion' with the critical and defensive mechanisms of the concrete mind, rather than limiting it entirely to the dislikes and hatreds that are the direct opposite of

---

[1] p. 87, op. cit. The italics are mine.—G. C.

desire and lust, I am departing from the letter of most of the standard translations and commentaries,[1] but not, I think, from their spirit. They are fairly well agreed that the obstacle of aversion has to do with the sense of separateness and the negation of unity and brotherhood. It is a well-established psychological tenet that the emotion of hate is closely related to that of love, so much so that it is a common, perhaps a universal experience for a man to have flashes of hate toward those whom he most loves. Aversion, however, is allied with contempt and withdrawal. The brahmin does not 'hate' the pariah from whose shadow he withdraws himself; the French aristocrat did not 'hate' the canaille whom he spurned, nor the Pharisee the wounded and dirty traveller by the wayside when he passed him by with contemptuous indifference. For such reasons as these it would seem that while desire is primarily an emotional automatism, aversion is a mental one, and that the habit of destructive criticism and individualistic withdrawal is the obstacle implied by the term.

The fifth hindrance is translated as attachment, or clinging to life, and Patanjali says that this obstacle is 'found even in the wise' and is ever sustained by its own force. Here we are on familiar

[1] Alice Bailey appears to accept this view on p. 128 of her paraphrase, but somewhat negates it on p. 136. (*The Light of the Soul*, by A. A. Bailey, New York, 1927.)

ground, for this is the instinct of self-preservation, the will to live. Yet there is a very wide difference between the eastern and western outlook on the matter, for whereas in the west life is accounted good in spite of its miseries, in the east it is regarded as ill in spite of its illusory joys, and to escape from the wheel of reincarnation is the goal of effort. But although life in the physical world is to the yogi wholly undesirable, yet every living thing, including the yogi himself, has the instinct to prolong life, and this conflict is therefore one of the great hindrances on the path of yoga.

The question then arises whether these five obstacles—ignorance, self-esteem, desire, aversion, attachment to life—are in any sense fundamental and vital factors to be met with in the course of analytical treatment. It will probably be admitted by the analyst that most people who present themselves for analysis, however learned they may be in the pursuit of their several callings, are comprehensively ignorant of their own psychology. At the physical level they are unaware not only of the obvious causes of their own ill health and nervous exhaustion, but also of their bodily movements, their tics and tensions. It is quite usual for a patient under analysis to sit or recline with every muscle tense, to wring his hands, tap his foot, massage his mouth strenuously with his fingers, and yet be

completely unaware that he is making any movement or showing any signs of nervous stress. But
his physical unawareness is nothing in comparison
with his complete lack of mento-emotional self-consciousness and self-comprehension. He has for years
been the prey of emotions to which he cannot give
a name; afraid of he knows not what; depressed, he
knows not why; irritable without recognizing the
source of his irritation; deeply disturbed by sex impulses when he imagines himself to be so spiritually
minded or so intellectually absorbed that he has no
room for such commonplace grossness. Or, on the
other hand, he may picture himself as sexually
speaking a prince of sinners, when in reality he is
a blameless intellectual and a prude. He has standards of behaviour and sets of opinions which he has
always imagined to be his own, but which shortly
turn out to be the property of his grandfather, or of
the set of fellows he knew at college, or of his daily
paper. For, as our discussion of confused thinking
showed, the average man and woman lives in so
habitual a state of self-ignorance that when the analyst holds up a mirror the analysand indignantly
repudiates the image that appears therein, and not
infrequently makes off in high dudgeon and fails
to return. Unquestionably ignorance is a well-
recognized obstacle to the process of analysis.

In the early days of analytical therapy a relatively

small place was given in the literature of the subject
to what was known as narcissism. Certain auto-
erotic physical habits, normal in infancy, were described as narcissistic, and when they persisted in
later life it was noted that the person in question
had failed to make the normal transfer of emotional
interest from self and towards others, and was still
his own primary love-object. Of late years the question of narcissism has been receiving much greater
attention, and it is now regarded as a very important one. It is recognized that we do not outgrow
our infantile narcissism, but that it merely becomes
transformed into the universal self-love and self-
interest which is basic in human nature. In the
normal person attachment to outside objects or
object-love tends to balance self-love, but the adjustment is a delicate one and easily upset. Un-
balanced narcissism is obviously anti-social, and
hence public opinion demands that it shall be sup-
pressed and disguised; but we are seldom content
merely to deceive others in such matters, and must
needs for our greater comfort deceive also ourselves. Narcissus looking into a quiet pool fell in
love with his own perfections; and in order to remain comfortably in love with ourselves we must
needs see a pleasing reflection when we look into
our pool. Humanity is not perfect, and if the reflection were faultless we could not but doubt it; so we

arrange to see in ourselves a few of the more respectable faults, such as anger, extravagance, laziness, thoughtlessness, but avoid seeing selfishness, meanness, greed, and the like. As a result an early and persistent obstacle in analysis is the resistance of the patient to face such motives and patterns of living as are damaging to his self-esteem. Wherever a strongly established family or caste tradition is presumed to require one type of motive, it is extremely difficult to face in one's self the existence of something hostile to it. Thus in a family where there is a strong tradition of social service and altruism, it is shameful not to 'feel' the wrongs of the oppressed, and to be merely bored with them is unspeakable. Where hunting and shooting and sport are traditional, physical cowardice is the thing that cannot be admitted, whereas lack of interest in humanitarian schemes may be taken for granted. Hence self-love is often so closely bound up with the approbation of our fellows that we esteem ourselves for the qualities which our environment considers valuable.

Another manifestation of self-esteem or narcissism commonly met with as a serious obstacle in analytic treatment is the fantasy or picture of one's self as the centre round which cause and effect and the happenings of life are grouped. There is a natural tendency to wish and even to expect that the events of life, the plans of other people, the hours at which trains or other conveyances depart and arrive, the weather and so forth should be arranged to suit ourselves; and we daily feel and express annoyance that it is not so. This is one of the major fantasies that prevent the average person from adapting himself to life. A further neurotic development of the same automatism is the conviction that life is deliberately arranged to thwart us, and that circumstances are united to bring about our undoing. It is well known that this type of fantasy verges on mania, and easily develops into an incurable psychosis.

What Patanjali calls the obstacle of desire is met with and recognized by the analyst in the inability of the patient to disentangle himself from his own emotional experience. There is no doubt that feeling, whether nominally painful or pleasurable, is definitely enjoyable, and that there is an ever-present tendency to linger in it and to savour it. The analyst's chief protection against this form of dalliance is his fee, and the fact that the customary hour or fifty minutes' interview ends sternly by the clock. But apart from the enjoyment of emotion there is a deeper and more genuine difficulty consisting in the fact that the patient actually does still identify himself with situations that were once real but have at the present time no validity. The classic example of this is the way in which people live over and over again the miseries and tragedies of their childhood, with affect that was appropriate then but is irrational now. Thus an adult at an analytical interview will bring himself (or herself), with the utmost difficulty and with every mark of abject shame and distress, to admit that when a child he once stole pennies from the mantelpiece or hit his sister over the head so as to make her cry, and then denied that he had done it. The reality attitude toward such incidents is one of detachment, for in fact the man has long since outgrown the desire to steal pennies and ill-treat babies; but the emotion that surrounded those deeds in childhood has never been disintegrated, because the man has never objectified his own childhood.

The fantastic identification of the self with emotional experience is by no means confined to such early memories. It is usual for a person to be so involved in the emotions of the moment as to be incapable of seeing the true bearings of any given situation. The man or woman who is in love or in a temper cannot control the emotion so long as he or she is *in* it; a withdrawal and a reference to the self as the experiencer and the emotion as objective experience is first necessary, and both yoga and analysis tend to bring about this withdrawal, this disentanglement.

Aversion, or hostile withdrawal from objects in

one's environment, is in ordinary life the great obstacle or hindrance to social adaptation. The process of analysis if successful brings about many
forms of adaptation, differing in different cases.
There is the adjustment to the self brought about
mainly through emotional self-awareness, the adjustment to sex and to various personal relationships, the adjustment to personal circumstances of
occupation and surroundings, the adjustment to
the community with the necessity for fellowship
and reciprocity, and the big adjustment to life itself
which involves all the others and yet goes beyond
them. These various adaptations, of which only
some outstanding ones have been enumerated, are
not really separate items in a series, but are so inter-
related in practice as to be indistinguishable; yet in
any given analysis it is usual for at least one or two
of them to be of special significance. Whereas the
Freudian analyst has laid great stress on the need
for adaptation to reality in sexual experience, the
Adlerian emphasis has been and is laid on the need
for social adaptation. Although the obstacles of
Patanjali are, like the Freudian mechanisms, universal and not sporadic in their validity, yet in
different types of people one will expect to find
different ones predominating. I think it may be
said that aversion is particularly an obstacle of the
mentally over-active rather than of the obviously

emotional type. By this I mean an individual not necessarily lacking in emotional capacity, but in whom emotional retreat has been compensated for by mental development. When a child is for any reason unsatisfied and unsuccessful in its adaptation to life it usually adopts one of two courses. Either it devises some scheme or subterfuge for attaining its desire, or else it withdraws and, unable to face the pain and sense of insecurity arising from the unsatisfied wish, pretends to itself and to its world that it really wants something different *and superior*. Like the fox in the fable it affects scorn and aversion for the grapes it cannot reach, or, as in the other less well-known folk story, having lost its own brush by an accident it makes a great talk about the ugliness, uselessness, and inconvenience of tails in general, and the superiority of the person who lacks such an appendage. In this way the attitude of critical disparagement gets a strong hold on the personality, colours the whole attitude to life, and produces an anti-social pattern leading in after-life to acute maladaptation and neurosis. Thus the person who in childhood has been for any reason frustrated in social adaptation, it may be through the handicap of bodily infirmity, through poverty, or through a variety of other causes, feels himself bereft, insecure, and inferior. If in seeking some way of avoiding this painful situation he hits on a form of mental superiority which wins him much coveted adult applause and approbation, this is likely to determine his life-pattern. He becomes the wit or the 'brainy one of the family', and wins for himself exemption from the social side of life in which he has failed to shine. He excels at school, and the family, seeing in him a possible scholarship-winner, makes what provision it can to exclude him from the rough and tumble of family life in order that he may have opportunity for study. This does not make the child happy, because people are never happy in evading reality-adaptation, and he some-how knows it is an evasion although the family may not. But he does feel for the moment secure from the ridicule and mortified vanity that his social in-feriority brings upon him, and so accepts the evasion. This is an elementary example of a character in which aversion is cultivated as a defence mechan-ism. The analyst has to deal with cases far more intricate and elusive.

Another common type is that of the compulsive talker who never stops talking long enough to allow himself or herself any social intercourse. The talk-ing is a barrage against feeling and against being 'got at'. Because agreeable and fluent conversation is an accepted outward mark of social success, the compulsive talker is able to picture himself as doing the correct thing and so to satisfy his self-esteem.

Such people are not conscious of the fact that they never make contact with others, and are unaware that their conversations are monologues.

Attachment, or the will to live, is definitely recognized by the yogi as an undesirable quality, though inevitable. The analyst regards the will to live as neither desirable nor undesirable, but merely as a universal and necessary fact. But he recognizes that it is a fact on which the whole analytical structure is based. Modern analytical therapy regards insecurity and anxiety as the fundamental cause of all neurosis, and the aim of the analyst is to open up the unconscious anxieties of his patient and discover their cause. Anxiety may be due to fear of the unknown, fear of what is going to happen next, dread that the future holds some terrible retribution— that the wolf will eat little Red Riding Hood, who is Me, or that the tigers will devour little Black Sambo.[1] Fairy-tales are full of these awful catastrophes that have to be averted by magic or agility or ready wit. The childish compulsion-games which in pre-analytic days were regarded as being 'just the funny things that children do'—you must touch every lamp-post, you must never step on a crack, you must find a lucky stone on the beach, or something dark and terrible will happen—are all alike

[1] As Jung has shown, myths and fairy-tales are often symbolic pictures of the unconscious mind.

evidences of the fear of the unknown, which is really a sense of the uncertainty of life, imbedded in us and showing itself from earliest babyhood. As we grow older it manifests itself in a great many ways, but especially in fear of change and growth—in a hundred fears that are all the same fear, namely that we shall not have the things, objective or subjective, which we consider necessities of life, and that failing them we shall 'die' either literally or by implication. Hence we cling desperately to the outgrown or outworn form or formula, to any sort of prop that has made life tolerable—it may be a physical environment, a house, a home, a circle of friends; it may be a fantasy which seems to us more tolerable than stark reality. To put the matter differently: human consciousness at the present time, whether owing to education or to its stage of social development, tends to demand a fixed standard, to seek the familiar and to avoid the unknown. People ask that life shall be absolute in values, and shall not take them unawares. Relativity, however, is of the essence of life. Life moves, changes inevitably, and the unexpected and the unknown are always coming upon us. Owing to ignorance there is in every man a deep resistance to life as life, an incapacity to accept the flow of things and adapt to it freely. It is sitting loose to life, accepting it as it comes rather than demanding from it what you expect, that both analyst and yogi regard as constituting the 'free psyche', 'liberation', which in the eyes of both is the pearl of great price worth any sacrifice to attain.

In the early days of psychotherapy it was customary to talk about a person as being 'fully analysed' when a satisfactory analysis was completed, and if this were still the case it would be necessary to remind oneself at this point that the yogi's idea of liberation goes so far beyond the analyst's conception of a 'free psyche' that the two are not really comparable. The analyst of to-day has, however, abandoned the idea of a complete analysis as being at our present stage unrealizable. He expects from analysis 'a greater reality-sense, and a greater ability to operate in reality with less anxiety and greater satisfaction, ... the greater possibility of an integrated purpose in life, and much greater power of being emotionally unperturbed by the hostility and the affects of other people',[1] and he expects much wider results in time to come, when analytical knowledge and technique have progressed further. This increased measure of freedom and integrity of purpose is precisely what is looked for in the early stages of yoga. Analytical therapy in the west is a very new and young experiment, yoga

[1] 'The Technique of Psycho-analysis', by E. F. Sharpe, *International Journal of Psycho-analysis*, vol. xi, Part 4, Oct. 1930.

in the east is a very ancient and mature technique. Hence the resemblances that we may hope to find between the two are likely to concern what is known as preliminary yoga. Whether the trend of analytical therapy is in the same direction as that of advanced yoga must be a more or less speculative question.[1]

[1] Cf. op. cit., vol. xii, Part I, p. 25.

Chapter XI

OVERCOMING THE OBSTACLES: THE FIVE PRELIMINARY EXERCISES

HAVING enumerated and explained the five obstacles to yoga, Patanjali states that there are
eight exercises or practices which assist in overcoming them.[1] Of these the first four are means
of dealing with the problems of everyday life, the
control of the body and the senses; the last
three are exercises in meditation or conscious
samādhi (see p. 103), and the fifth is for the purpose
of raising consciousness from its ordinary state
to that of concentration or meditation. It is
proposed in this chapter to deal with the first
five of these, and more especially with the first
two, which are of considerable significance to the
western psychologist.

The five have been rendered as follows:[2]

1. The practice of harmlessness, i.e. obedience
   to the moral law.
2. Discipline, i.e. obedience to the spiritual
   law.
3. Posture or poise.
4. The regulation of breath.
5. Withdrawal or abstraction.

[1] II. 29–55.   [2] II. 29.

Harmlessness is said to include abstention from lying, stealing, incontinence, and covetousness or greed, and this law is of universal obligation.[1] In five subsequent sutras (35–9) the subtler implications of harmlessness are set forth and the results of obedience to the moral law enumerated.

The underlying idea of these five sutras is that in altering himself a man cannot fail to alter his environment. The sankhyan philosophy recognizes all life as having one source,[2] and hence considers that the consciousness of the yogi is fundamentally one with that of his environment. It follows therefore that by altering himself he alters what might be called an ingredient in the universe, and this modification of the universe within himself necessarily reacts upon that with which it is most closely associated, namely his immediate surroundings. This fact is well evidenced in psychological practice, but the sequence of events is there generally considered to be that the person who changes his character in so doing develops within himself power to control his circumstances more skilfully. Both statements appear to be accurate.

The spiritual discipline consists of purification, contentment, and the three preliminary attitudes

---

[1] II. 30–1.
[2] A theory to which modern science would probably assent if the one source were taken to be solar energy.

or exercises with which we are already familiar, namely mortification or discipline, study, and resignation to God.[1]

It is not necessary to repeat here what has already been said about these three preliminary exercises and the reasons for their importance in yoga. They involve attitudes of mind which are inherent in the method, and which are of permanent as well as of preliminary value. But here two further requirements are added to the three already given. The reader may have noticed the tendency to see all these considerations relating to yoga in five aspects or facets. Thus there are five obstacles, five exercises for overcoming them, the moral law has five subdivisions, and the spiritual discipline when given in full is fivefold, not threefold. The reason for this tendency is probably to be found in the conception of man as a fivefold being (see pp. 95 et seq.), for examination shows that each of the five aspects bears a specific relation to an element in man's consciousness. It is not necessary to go into detail here as regards these fivefold correspondences, but in the sutra under discussion one may observe that purification bears special relation to the physical, contentment to the emotional, and mortification or discipline to the concrete mind, since mortification involves a loosening and relinquishing of fixity and

[1] II. 32.

mental automatisms; study relates to the higher mental faculties, and resignation to Ishvara to the use of the will.

The question of posture or poise is one that has a far wider significance to the eastern student than it has in the west, for no one can live in any country where yoga is extensively practised without being aware of the strange and elaborate system of posture which forms so large a part of the training of Hatha Yoga, one of the seven schools referred to previously (see p. 10). The disciple of this school spends much time in acquiring a series of movements and positions of the body of such a nature that a western acrobat would be hard put to it to imitate them. Therefore when Patanjali says that in the Raja Yoga system of which he is the exponent the position for meditation should merely be easy and steady[1] he is stating a point of view that would not be by any means acceptable to all schools of thought in the east. He goes on to say in the two sutras following this that although violent contortions are neither necessary nor desirable, yet it is essential to accustom the body to some one position which is easy and poised, and that until this is done it is not possible to proceed to actual meditation.

The fourth preliminary exercise is that of prāna-yāma or breath-control. The eastern student is

[1] II. 46.

taught that breathing exercises give him a control of the life-force or nervous energy of the body,[1] and that as this control is obtained certain faculties can be awakened, certain nerve centres vivified, which enable him to gain mastery over subtler forms of consciousness.

Exercises in breath-control are accompanied by efforts to withdraw the consciousness from sense contacts, so that it may attain to a state of pure thought. The disciple is taught to observe his sensory experiences carefully and then to delete them at will (hearing a clock ticking and then refusing to hear it, &c.), and thus to realize his consciousness as able to function apart from sensory phenomena in a condition of mental abstraction. This is the fifth preliminary exercise, which we have rendered 'abstraction', and we are told (in II. 54, 55) that this, the last of the preliminary exercises, leads to such control of the senses as makes them no longer a hindrance but an invaluable help in meditation.

From this brief outline of the five preliminary exercises it appears that two are concerned with forms of moral and spiritual training such as are familiar enough in the west, while three are technical practices calculated to produce a certain state of consciousness, and unfamiliar to the western student. Obviously these last three in their technical sense

[1] See p. 119.

have no relationship to western psychotherapy as generally practised, although it is conceivable that the time may come when the value of regulated breath, sustained poise, and a deliberate objectifying and rendering aware of sense contacts may become a recognized technique among psychotherapists in dealing with certain types of neurosis. As yet this is not the case, and hence it is not relevant to discuss these three practices here.

The question of moral and spiritual training required in the student of yoga is of more immediate relevance, since the attitude of the analyst to moral education has long been a matter of controversy among psychologists. The position of the yogi in regard to moral and spiritual discipline is a logical and not a sentimental one. The serious and successful practice of yoga gives to the student powers greatly exceeding those of his fellow-men, and these can be used to the advantage or to the detriment of the community. Setting aside the question of supernormal faculties, the very fact that a yogi has far greater self-control and deeper insight than the ordinary man puts at his command forces which can be used for selfish ends and to dominate his fellows. Hence it is obviously desirable for the good of the community that he should be as far as possible incapable of so misusing them.

In the west it is proverbial that knowledge is

power, and probably most people would if challenged acquiesce in the statement that it should therefore be linked with a sense of moral responsibility. We are beginning to admit that posts of responsibility should be given to those who have expert knowledge, but the point of view that a high standard of morality ought to be exacted from the man to whom the great power of specialized knowledge is committed or permitted has been foreign to our way of thinking. In this respect as in so many others the east differs from the west, and hence we should not expect to find in analytical therapy the same kind of emphasis on moral training and spiritual discipline as is found in yoga training. In the west there is a large section of public opinion that values morality and spirituality for their own sake, and for the happiness that they are believed to bring to the individual and to the community; but the conception that this or that piece of knowledge and understanding should be withheld from a man until his moral and spiritual standards are such as make him unlikely to misuse it for his own ends is not only unfamiliar but definitely uncongenial to our western mind. The distinction between esoteric and exoteric knowledge is one that is looked upon askance by the European as somewhat fantastic and wholly undesirable.

It is conceivable that in future ages we may come

to realize that analytical treatment, if at all completely carried out, may give to the person who undergoes it so great an increase of power in himself and understanding of his fellows as to make him a source of possible danger to the community if he be inclined to misuse his capacities. This is no idle fantasy, for the admitted object of analysis is to set free libido or energy and to teach the analysand to understand the workings of the psychic mechanism; and it would be universally admitted that a free flow of psychic energy and a subtle knowledge of human nature are among the most powerful tools for self-advancement that a human being can possess. But be this as it may, at the present time this particular aspect of the moral responsibility of the analyst to the community is not widely recognized. The analyst's responsibility is toward the individual whom he is treating and from whom he is taking payment, and it is from this point of view that the question of moral and spiritual training has to be regarded.

We have now to consider whether the psychotherapist at the present day has an adequate technique for dealing with the problem of the person who desires through analysis to tackle difficulties of character and not merely those of health, or whether something of the training we have been discussing could be advantageously included in psychological treatment.

The earlier analysts considered that all psychological confusions and inhibitions were removed by externalization, and that when the patient had brought into consciousness and realized mentally and emotionally the root of his difficulties they ceased to exist, and the stream of vital energy thus freed was sufficient to enable him to deal with his problems. The result was therefore a restoration of health of mind and physical well-being. The modern analyst realizes that while this is often true it is by no means always so. He is confronted with an ever-widening range of human problems, and his technique is becoming more flexible and adaptable as need arises. There are cases where the character and temperament of the patient are such that, having in the process of analysis recognized his difficulties, he can without further assistance from the analyst, make his own adaptations to life; there are also a great many instances where the bringing to the surface of unconscious material does not give the necessary release. It may be that the patient is too near the border-line of what we call insanity, or that he or she is an hysterical type and lacks the capacity to bring the will into play in dealing with the situation; it may be that past experience has been of so prolonged or shattering a nature that the whole personality is disintegrated and has lost its normal power of psychic and physical recuperation. In any of these circumstances to continue to press purely reductive analysis may do more harm than good, and this many analysts have of late years discovered.

It is now some time since Ferenczi demonstrated the advisability in certain cases and at certain moments of departing from the strict Freudian attitude of non-interference and passivity and of adopting measures which involved regulating the patient's conduct in this direction or in that. This interference was of a purely temporary nature and had no moral implications. Thus the patient might be asked to abstain from reading certain books, or from discussing his analytical treatment with a friend, or from sexual intercourse for a certain period, the object being merely that of intensifying the analytical situation and so hastening the progress of the treatment. Nevertheless, the acceptance of the principle of active intervention on the part of the Freudian school marked a definite epoch in that branch of psychotherapy. The Jungians and Adlerians have from the first differed from the Freudians in regard to the educative function of the analyst, and have been definitely in favour of giving to the patient such moral and social re-education as he may be willing to accept. Their view is that one main object of analytical therapy is to enable the patient to adapt himself to his social environment.

Since a necessary factor in such adaptation is the acceptance of certain standards of behaviour, it follows that this acceptance should be aided in every possible way; hence the social groups of the Adlerians, and their interest in political reform. The Freudian admits the validity of social adaptation, but considers that if standards of morality be inculcated from without they become merely compulsive and imitative, and that the function of the analyst is to analyse, not to reinforce compulsive behaviour.

To give up alcohol or gambling because it is advantageous to oneself and fits into a chosen plan of life and not in response to the compulsion of conscience or of the super-ego, to practise generosity or continence as a self-determined activity and not from motives of fear or self-esteem, is to act in accordance with the precepts of yoga and also of psychotherapy. But the vast importance of this interior distinction between compulsive and self-determined activity is seldom clearly recognized, though it is basic. Where any training comparable to that of yoga is undertaken by a western student it is nearly always with a religious motive, and the discipline is followed in a spirit of conscientious obligation in which the confusion between free choice and compulsive adherence to an external pattern is hard to disentangle. To omit or fall short in such religious exercises is usually regarded as a spiritual backsliding or a sin against God, and hence strict adherence to the pattern is compelled by reverence or fear of sin. On the other hand, the person who genuinely wishes to become a skilled musician will perhaps practise six or eight hours a day regularly, it may be with fatigue, hardship, and self-denial; but he undergoes the discipline because he himself desires it, and if he omits his practising through laziness or self-indulgence he regards his omission as a folly and not as moral guiltiness. It is when undertaken from this latter point of view that yoga training becomes effective, and it is in this spirit that the analyst is prepared to accept moral discipline as valid.

The technique by which the patient can be instigated to embark upon self-determined activities is a subtle one, since direct advice must be avoided and the patient thrown upon his own resources. Although suggestion and even hypnotism are used by certain practitioners, these are in no sense analytical therapy. In the strictest sense any exercise suggested to the patient lies outside the range of analytical treatment. If however the whole matter of moral and social discipline, relaxation, breathing, and control of thought by meditation were approached by psychotherapists in the non-religious and scientific attitude of the student of yoga, it might well be that this would lead to the discovery of new and valuable psychotherapeutic methods.

This whole matter is so important that it will be further discussed from a slightly different angle in the chapter on suggestion and contrary production.

Chapter XII

OVERCOMING THE OBSTACLES:
CONCENTRATION

UP to the point reached in the previous chapter the material of preliminary yoga and the theory and technique of analytical therapy could be placed side by side and compared, but at this stage, namely at the beginning of Book III of the sutras, the science of yoga begins to pass beyond the confines of analytical therapy, so that the comparison tends to be between yoga and the future potentialities of that science.

Psychotherapy is a means of obtaining self-knowledge through breaking down the shell of fantasy in which the ordinary person is confined. At present this is the goal of analysis, and the analyst as a rule has nothing further to offer when that work has been achieved. Yet there are many cases which fail just because of this limitation, and there are also many where a successful analysis leaves the analysand high and dry because he is more than ever before conscious of demanding something further from life than it has yet given him and he does not in the least know where to look for it.[1] The yogi, however, considers the attainment of self-knowledge to be merely

---

[1] Cf. *A Soul in the Making* or *Psycho-synthesis*, by Dean Bennett of Chester Cathedral, who comments on this difficulty.

a preliminary step, not a goal but a gateway leading into a new country. To return to a figure used previously, the relative achievement of self-knowledge effected by an averagely successful analysis constitutes the lifting of the painted drop-curtain which hitherto formed an impenetrable barrier between the individual and the world of reality. This real world beyond is not easy to explore, and to perceive its existence is not necessarily to enter into the kingdom. But the science of yoga, having shown how the preliminary veil of illusion may be lifted, proceeds to a discussion of what lies beyond. The question that seems to be worth considering in our concluding chapters is whether the eastern method of exploring the beyond has any validity for the western student. Although a westerner can hardly expect to find in it directions and advice wholly suitable to the needs of an age and a race so widely different from that for which it was devised, yet it may well contain clues which will be of assistance in helping him to formulate his own scheme of approach.

Once more we need to remember that the eastern theory of mind is far more definite and clear-cut than that of the west. The conception of mind as a subtle substance having spatial existence and capable of taking on shape is so basic in eastern psychology and so foreign to the west that it constitutes a real barrier to mutual understanding; and when as at this juncture we come to deal with yoga theories of mind-training, the difference in point of view needs to be constantly borne in mind.

On the other hand, the yogi is in complete accord with the modern trend of western psychology which recognizes most of our thinking as being a defence and a flight from reality. 'The mind is the enemy of the real' is his way of putting it, and the first steps in actual yoga-practice, as distinct from preliminary exercises, are directed toward stilling busy-mindedness. They are an effort to quiet the waves and ripples of consciousness, and to produce a mirror-like surface in which reality can be reflected without distortion.

Let us then consider in some detail the early sutras of Book III, which deal with the practical question of mind-training and its results upon consciousness. If we recall here the opening sutras of Book I we shall see more clearly the point at which we have arrived.

'Yoga is attained by gaining complete mastery over the mind and the emotions. The individual then becomes aware of himself. Ordinarily he is identified with or lost in his own confused picture of life.... Yoga is attained by the control and ultimately the suppression at will of all forms of thinking. This is gained by determined and sustained effort coupled with increasing detachment and dispassion.'[1]

[1] I. 2, 3, 4, 12, 13.

Preliminary yoga has for its object the breaking up of the automatic and unaware habits of thought and feeling which make up the 'confused picture of life', and for this reason I have ventured to argue that preliminary yoga is an eastern equivalent of analytical therapy. When this process has been to some extent achieved—its complete achievement is a goal and not a preliminary step—the student of yoga sets about the further mastering of the mind by the study of concentration.

Book III opens with the statement that when concentration is undertaken, it is a definite process with three *stages* leading to a fourth *state*. In the first stage, which we have called concentration (see p. 122), a subject for thought is selected, and the task of controlling the more violent oscillations of the mind by the deleting of distractions is begun. At this stage four factors are present in consciousness: (1) the sense of self-direction, or the will, (2) the instrument of thought or the mind, (3) the object on which concentration is being attempted, (4) intrusive ideas or distractions.

There are two well-known methods of dealing with distractions. Some temperaments find it more satisfactory to force the mind into one-pointedness by a summary dismissal of all intruding images and ideas; others prefer the equally effective method of allowing the oscillations gradually to subside until the movement is such that it can be fairly easily controlled. In either case a distinct effort of will is necessary, but the technique is different.

In the second stage, which we have called deliberation, the fourth factor of intrusive ideas has been to a great extent eliminated, but three factors still remain in consciousness—the will or sense of self, the mind, and the object of thought. That is to say the process is still one of conscious effort. The student is aware that his power of self-direction is holding his mind steady upon an object. This is the period of maximum effort and distaste, at which the experiment very commonly breaks down.

In the third stage, which we have called contemplation, there is no longer consciousness of effort, and no longer awareness of the mind as an instrument, but simply awareness of the object of thought. The eastern way of expressing this is to say that the mind is now completely transformed into the object, or has taken on its shape.

These three stages lead to a fourth which is not a stage but an achieved condition of consciousness, and the transition to it from the third phase is a delicate and critical process because the state itself may take one of two forms. In its passive form it becomes a condition of mediumistic trance which is negative and unproductive and against which the student is warned.[1] The active form, which is positive and creative, is a profound tuning of the mind to the object of study, which results in deep insight and a tapping of a wide range of correlated ideas. It is this greatly increased capacity for seeing relationships which constitutes the most fruitful and practical aspect of the meditation exercise.

A little consideration seems to show that we have here once more the fourfold process of creative activity previously referred to—the selecting or fixing on the object, the effort to achieve union, the interval of suspense, and the creative climax.

The third stage, that of suspension, which is characterized by the cessation of effort, brings with it a feeling of poise, of floating, of 'being just about to', and is acutely pleasant but often very brief. It tends, as we have noted, to merge insensibly either into a state of dreamy passivity or into its true climax, a condition of intense activity which like all very rapid movement gives the impression of stillness. This final condition is accompanied by a sense of boundless power and capacity, a mastery of the subject in hand, and is a state of radiant expansion and fulfilment which resembles ecstasy and is yet more positive and active than what is usually meant by that word. The poet Tennyson describes the condition as follows:

[1] I. 19.

'A kind of waking trance I have frequently had, quite up from my boyhood, when I have been all alone. This has generally come upon me through repeating my own name two or three times to myself silently, till all at once, as it were out of the intensity of the consciousness of individuality, the individuality itself seemed to dissolve and fade away into boundless being; and this is not a confused state, but the clearest of the clearest, the surest of the surest, the weirdest of the weirdest, utterly beyond words, where death was an almost laughable impossibility, the loss of personality (if so it were) seeming no extinction, but the only true life. This might be the state which St. Paul describes, "Whether in the body I cannot tell, or whether out of the body I cannot tell".'

So pleasurable are these later stages of concentration that the yoga sutras repeatedly warn the student against resting content with an achievement of conscious samādhi and failing therefore to attain the ultimate goal of yoga.

The question arises why so intensely pleasurable an activity is not more widely practised and achieved, since there is no obvious barrier that prevents any one who chooses from making the effort. There seem to be various answers to this question. In the first place, the majority of mankind do experience its equivalent at the physical level, for the sexual creative act is admittedly the supreme and most desired gratification of the senses, and is an exact counterpart of the mental and spiritual creative processes of which, as the east maintains, it is merely the reflection. There is in sexual life a selection of and fixing upon an object, a period of effort to become identified with and united to the beloved, a longer or shorter period of suspense and sustained excitement, and a creative climax. The obviousness of the creative result, that is the conception of a child, a new physical form, is a matter of enormous pride and self-satisfaction. It is a direct and undeniable achievement. That it has a true counterpart at the mental level in the effort of union with a new idea, in the release of creative excitement that comes with a deep and comprehending grasp of a new concept, has hardly occurred to the majority of mankind. They are content with the immediate personal and physical experience, and seek nothing further. The fact that the physical satisfaction of sex-intercourse in itself, apart from procreation, is admittedly transient is regarded in the east as an ordinance of nature, designed that man may be led to seek the more sustained delight of mental and spiritual creative effort. St. Augustine states the same thing from the Christian viewpoint: 'Thou hast made of us for Thyself; and the heart is ever restless till it finds its rest in Thee.' That mental creation is more satisfying and compelling than physical would be admitted by many artists, who reckon toil. hardship, and the sacrifice of much that to other men makes life worth living as of small account beside the joy of achievement.

Nevertheless, it is true that a very small proportion of mankind are aware of the possibilities of the type of mental experience that we are discussing, and of these only a few actually achieve it in any recognizable degree. The reason for this is well known to all who have ever attempted any form of deliberate meditation, namely that the early stages are as irksome as the later stages are pleasurable. Any religious manual on meditation will supply a description of the boredom and sense of inability and hopelessness, accompanied often by a peculiarly unbearable form of restlessness, which daunt the beginner and which may for a long time constitute his sole experience. The capacity for persistent effort in the face of apparently insurmountable difficulty is always rare, but pre-eminently so at the mental level. Patanjali goes on to say,[1] as do the Christian manuals, that by habitual practice the difficulty of the first and second stages is gradually overcome, so that the mind is able to reach and to sustain the one-pointed or poised condition at will, and to proceed confidently from it to the creative state.

The secret is the attaining of balance (sattva) between two inherent tendencies of the mind, the

[1] III. 10.

inert (tamasic) on the one hand and the active (rajasic) on the other. Over-activity, the flitting from one thing to another, prevents creativeness, but so equally does inertia, dullness, unwillingness to move.[1]

Poise at a third point, which neutralizes the swing from one extreme to the other, is the result of equal detachment from both, and an equal capacity to be at rest or active, interested or withdrawn at will. Here we meet the familiar teaching in regard to the pairs of opposites, in this case applied to mental experience. The sankhyan psychology, being founded on the triplicities of matter and spirit, constantly falls back upon the idea that release from this or that obstacle is attained by achieving a harmonized or sattvic condition of consciousness in regard to each. Psychotherapists are fully aware of the working out of this theory in practice. The patient who swings from deep self-love into equal self-hate has to discard both attitudes, and arrive at a third and novel view of himself as neither the best nor the worst person in the world, but just an average maker of ordinary mistakes. The person who desires to be in the limelight and dresses with meticulous care yet takes the seat nearest the door 'to avoid being conspicuous' has to see both these conditions as equally unsound, and achieve

[1] III. 11 and 12.

a third condition of being willing to take a convenient place in the room, or in life, as occasion demands.

So with the inertia and over-activity of the mind; the student is expected to observe these opposites in mental tendency, and with practice and persistence to acquire skill in holding the mind itself calm, like the surface of a lake unclouded by mist and unruffled by wind. When such mental poise or complete mastery of thought is attained it becomes possible for the mind to perceive the fundamental nature of things and hence the seer (purusha) can both understand and control them.

The remainder of Book III is chiefly concerned with an enumeration of various manifestations of the gunas which can be dominated by samyāma,[1] the closing sutras containing the usual reminder that samyāma and the powers it brings are not the yogi's goal, but merely a step toward the attainment of true liberation (kaivalya).

In looking at this question of samyāma, or training of the higher mental faculty, our concern here is to form an opinion as to whether these further steps in yoga have any practical application for the analyst. As we have seen, purely reductive analysis is not by any means always sufficient to enable the analysand to achieve self-direction, to think and to

III. 4 et seq.

live constructively. That human nature at its present stage of evolution is not quite so simple as the
early analyst supposed is not really surprising. The
creative principle in each person is not merely
instinctive, animalistic, self-seeking, or even herd-
conscious. Eastern psychologists envisage purusha,
the spirit, as a complex mechanism. (See chart,
p. 234). The creative principle is merely freed
by reductive analysis, and needs some system of
deliberate exercise for its further development.

What it would mean to the race and to the more
rapid growth of human happiness if some scientific
technique could be developed in the west to foster
adult creative thinking no one can tell, though the
last chapter will include some speculation upon
this point. Those who stand in the forefront of
modern educational theory are recognizing more
and more that herein lies the genuine secret of the
right training of youth. For those in whom the
concrete mind is already strong and active education is sound only in so far as it tends to develop a
creative faculty, and judged by this criterion nine-
tenths of education is conspicuously unsound. For
many years to come the analyst will have the task
of endeavouring to correct the blunders and in-
adequacies of the parent and the teacher. But if
analysis, which at the present day may be said to be
in full leaf, is to reach maturity as a system—to flower

and to bear valuable fruit for the coming generations—it would seem that it must develop some
further technique than that which it now possesses.
Such a technique is imperative if the adult student
wishes to attain to a poise and mastery comparable
with that described in the yoga sutras.

This would demand a high standard of attainment in the analyst of the future. It is already part of
the analytical tradition that only the person who
has himself undergone the fullest possible experience
of analysis is equipped to use analytical therapy for
the benefit of others; and it has been said that the
analyst's mind must be as clean as the surgeon's
knife. But it would seem that the analyst of the
future should also be one who knows experiment-
ally something of the process of meditation, or the
obtaining of mastery of the mind, so that even if no
definite directions are asked for or given the analysand may feel for the analyst something of that
profound confidence, that sense of his capacity
for interior poise and spiritual insight, which the
aspirant to yoga is trained to recognize in his
teacher or guru.

Chapter XIII

SUGGESTION AND CONTRARY
PRODUCTION

O F late years the whole question of suggestion
as a psychological influence has been receiving
a long overdue measure of attention and recognition both in reference to the causation of disease
and as a method of healing; in other words the
great influence of the mind over the body has begun
to be recognized. Half a century ago the idea that
the mind had power over the functions and diseases
of the body was regarded as laughable; to-day it is
generally accepted as a fact, though its implications are still largely neglected. Hysteria is now
studied seriously as a form of neurosis, and the
notion that it is a purely feminine ailment and can
be banished by a judicious use of firmness and cold
water is no longer fully accepted. It is realized that
in men and women physical symptoms can be due
to a state of mind and that the alteration of the state
of mind may be in itself sufficient to relieve the
symptom. The success of various kinds of mental
healing and the widespread popular interest in the
work of Monsieur Coué helped to bring the whole
subject not merely into notice but into the limelight. The discovery, more or less fortuitous, that

analytical therapy could be effective in curing not only neuroses but also diseases that had been regarded as purely physical was a further stimulus to interest in the potency of the mind as a factor in healing. Hence no discussion of psychotherapy can wholly omit a consideration of the subject of suggestion, and it will be found that in preliminary yoga also it is a matter of some importance.

Book II of Patanjali contains the following sutra: 'In order to eradicate undesirable thoughts, habits of mind, and emotions, the student is recommended to meditate on their opposite. This eradication is valuable not only because it makes for progress in yoga, but also because it minimizes ill results' (i.e. the inevitable ill results of entertaining undesirable thoughts).[1]

The idea thus expressed is that the student of yoga who wishes to alter his characteristics or habits can do so by keeping his mind resolutely fixed on the opposite habit or characteristic. This would seem, for various reasons, to be a sound idea, and yet from another point of view it might well set up a query in the mind of the analyst. On the one hand it is admitted that thought is the forerunner of action, and if one can succeed in establishing a given train of thought with vigour and consistency one is likely to act in accordance with it even in an

[1] II. 34.

emergency. Again, Monsieur Coué and his followers have seemed to demonstrate that by auto-suggestion one can touch the unconscious layers of the mind and thereby alter not only conscious actions but unconscious automatisms.

The Coué method of auto-suggestion was to occupy the last moments between waking and sleeping in repeating aloud monotonously some formula suggesting the effect desired. When Coué himself used his method with the patients who flocked to Nancy to be treated by him, his procedure was first to bring the group into a state of complete acquiescence and passivity closely approximating to the relaxation that in most people precedes sleep, and then to make them repeat their formula, always insisting that this be done without effort or conscious desire, but as drowsily and mechanically as possible. In other words he brought his patients into a state of openness and acquiescence in which their ordinary resistances and inhibitions ceased for the moment to function, and by this means got behind their automatic defences without troubling to break these down. With certain temperaments the method produced miraculously quick results. But, as might have been expected, in many cases these proved to be purely superficial; for it was the barriers and inhibitions that produced the symptoms, and in so far as these barriers remained untouched they tended to produce fresh symptoms when the interest and impetus of the Coué treatment had subsided. For this reason the analyst did not accept Coué's method with unreserved enthusiasm, and yet the fact that it produced definitely successful results would indicate that 'contrary production' or meditation on the opposite is to some extent a valid technique.

But there is much to be said as to its dangers and pitfalls. The analyst is abundantly aware that compulsive standards of behaviour accepted from without, and auto-suggested and persevered in contrary to the natural desires, are one of the chief sources of the harmful 'repressions' about which the layman hears so much. The person who has taught himself to behave in a way that is not a sincere expression of his own nature has merely erected a façade behind which to hide, an ornamental piece of architecture intended to give a favourable impression to the world and to himself.

This cogent argument against the idea of contrary production is strengthened by the fact that a considerable number of western students who have been interested in yoga and have seriously used this method as a means of altering habits and character have been cramped and stultified rather than aided by the practice. It would seem to follow either that that method of contrary production is a fundamentally unsound one or else that it lends itself to misuse if imperfectly understood.

A closer examination of available evidence does tend to show that the process of 'meditating on the opposite' is a less simple matter than it seems and is beset by various pitfalls. In the preceding chapter the danger of setting out to live according to a fixed standard was seen to lie in the hidden nature of the motivation. If such a standard is maintained from a sense of exterior compulsion it is definitely harmful and stultifying to the development, and the degree of detachment and self-understanding required to distinguish between true self-determination and the urge of self-esteem, the desire to stand well with one's associates, or the fear of being isolated and ostracized, is considerable.

Another fundamental difficulty in the practice of contrary production is that of finding out what is in fact the true opposite and hence the effective antidote to any given bad habit or undesirable trait. I would go so far as to say that only rarely is a person able to see for himself wherein lies the true positive of his negative. The usual habit among people who attempt this method of self-discipline is to try to cultivate what I might call the verbal rather than the psychologically indicated opposite. This is due to our habit of thinking in dualities only and not as the east does in triplicities, whereas the true or effective 'opposite' is always the third quality, the sattvic or harmonizing third which resolves the dissonances. Thus the drunkard will perhaps try to hold before himself the beauty of temperance, the person subject to violent outbursts of temper will aspire to self-control and calmness, and the jealous person often tries to feel more loving. But there are many different causes for drunkenness, for bad temper, and even for jealousy. Drunkenness may be a form of gluttony, a desire for pleasurable sensation; but very often drink is used as an antidote for timidity and diffidence, or as a means of counteracting depression, and in such cases it is not temperance but self-confidence and courage that are the 'opposite' to be meditated upon. Outbursts of temper may result from selfish indifference and brutality of nature, but quite as often they are the indirect result of thwarted instincts, long-continued repression, over-conscientiousness, nervous hypersensitivity; and for the thwarted, hypersensitive person to meditate upon calmness and self-control is to evade the whole issue. Similarly the opposite of jealousy may be not love, but generosity or confidence and security. Hence the value and the success of this method depend on an insight and a self-knowledge that are rare; and whereas the yogi advised by the teacher who is training him, or the analysand in the hands of a competent analyst, could probably use it to great advantage, it has dangers for the unaided student.

It may here be of interest to conclude by giving a brief outline of the technique of contrary production as used by students of yoga. It is popularly understood that this technique demands a persistent assertion, audible or otherwise, of that which you do not believe to be true. Thus a timid elderly gentleman sitting in the back seat of a car driven by a speed-loving friend was heard to be engaged in a continuous but inaudible muttering. As the speed increased the murmurings became more agitated and more audible. A sudden lurch of the car precipitated a crisis, and the passenger was heard to exclaim in agony, 'God is love, and no harm can touch his child—*for God's sake, Arthur, drive a little slower!*'

The method when correctly employed is as follows: Let us suppose that a person realizes that he is vindictive, and wishes to alter this characteristic. It is almost impossible for any one who feels definitely vindictive to jump from that state of mind to one of active goodwill, but by cultivating some more general quality which is in a deep sense opposite and not merely contradictory, he can undermine his vicious tendency. In his case it has perhaps been shown that vindictiveness is a use of power to inflict pain, and that gentleness is its valid opposite. Having determined to eliminate vindictiveness he begins by making a close study of gentleness in all the variety of its manifestations—the feeble gentleness which goes with timidity, the courteous gentleness of the well-mannered, the sublime gentleness of the saint, which is a mixture of patience, tolerance, and power held in reserve. Thus he builds up an attraction toward the new quality, and his mind tends to flow into this pattern more and more readily. He continues to deliberate daily for some minutes upon the quality, and takes every opportunity of expressing it in practice. His experience, as evidenced by many who have tried the experiment, is likely to be as follows: First he becomes acutely aware as never before of his automatic vindictiveness. Then there is a period in which the automatic trend is partly offset by the deliberately induced habit.[1] If he is sufficiently determined and persevering his persistence of will can break up and really destroy the old condition. He will find that even in provocative circumstances the tendency to vindictiveness does not recur. It is of course obvious that to produce a profound change in character such as this will take a considerable time, and that many people who attempt it will lack the necessary staying power.

Contrary production practised in this way is a definite process of character-building and is neither

[1] See I. 14.

superficial nor unsound. To it, however, two sound objections can be raised. One, as has just been stated, is that it requires a capacity for sustained effort of will. From the yogi's point of view this is an advantage, not a drawback, since training of will-power is one of his main objects. The other difficulty is that deep unconscious fixations occasionally remain imbedded, particularly it would seem in the more rigid western type of mind, and these are so hostile and so unrealized that they may prevent achievement.

The question of the analyst's use of suggestion and hypnosis in his treatment is obviously closely allied to that of contrary production. In the early days of analytical therapy hypnosis was definitely part of the analyst's technique, and Freud himself employed it habitually. He soon became convinced that it was wholly unsound. The yogi would never use it with his pupils, because it attacks the self-command of the subject, nor does the present-day analyst for somewhat similar reasons do so, under ordinary circumstances. Some psychotherapists indeed make use of it either to get at deeply buried material, which can then be brought into waking consciousness by various methods such as post-hypnotic suggestion, or else to induce temporary control in cases of insomnia, drug-taking, drink, with the hope of thus setting up a contrary habit.

It is also used in treating some types of insanity, where the mental derangement is of such a nature that the patient cannot give conscious attention.

Hypnosis, while it is often confused with suggestion, is of course not at all the same thing. As to suggestion, in the ordinary sense of the word, every analyst uses this both consciously and unconsciously, and cannot possibly avoid doing so. His very existence as an analyst is in itself a powerful suggestion. In the course of treatment it is quite usual to suggest to the analysand such and such an interpretation of a dream, or to point out to him that certain material which comes up is particularly significant, and in so doing the analyst may, whether rightly or wrongly, influence the whole subsequent trend of the analysis. To say that this does not constitute a powerful suggestion is absurd. It may serve a useful purpose, but where the analyst hits upon and proceeds to emphasize one given line of interpretation to the exclusion of others it may equally be very damaging.

As to conscious and deliberate suggestion, the less rigid schools of analysis use it frankly and freely in given cases. Social activities and creative occupations are recommended, handicraft of various kinds is advised and often provided, and when circumstances permit the patient's entire mode of life may for the time be regulated and arranged for him.

One is forced to the conclusion that whatever may be the theoretical arguments for and against the use of suggestion in analysis, the fact remains that it plays and must play a considerable part in all such treatment; and it is a question whether the analyst would not do well to face this fact and devise a suitable and conscious technique for its application, rather than, as is often the case, maintain the fiction that the patient is entirely self-directing, and the analyst merely a passive listener.

Chapter XIV

THE SEER AND THE SEEN

Book IV of the yoga sutras is a metaphysical discussion of the nature of the self, the seer or purusha, and its relation to the seen, or the world of external phenomena.

The fundamental conception on which all yoga is based is that purusha, spirit (or the spirit), is immersed in and identified with the phenomenal world, and being so immersed is unable to realize itself. The cause of this identification is ignorance, and the task of the spirit or seer is to win freedom from the bondage of the external world by overcoming ignorance and all the obstacles and delusions arising therefrom. When the seer has finally accomplished this task, he is said to have attained complete liberation or kaivalya.

The seer looks at or cognizes external phenomena through the medium of the mind, and the yogi attains liberation by becoming fully and persistently awake to the inherent relation between the three factors, spirit, mind, and the external. The attainment of such awareness is progressive and gradual. In its earlier stages it consists in rendering conscious and controlling the mento-emotional automatisms which make up the greater part of the life of the ordinary man, and directions for doing this are given in Books I and II of the sutras. The object of analytical therapy is similar, namely to attain awareness and control.

A further degree of understanding of the relationship between spirit, mind, and the external world is obtained by the practice of samyāma (see pp. 120 et seq.) as described in Book III, and this leads to the development of higher and unusual faculties of consciousness which enable the yogi to behave in such a way that he appears to be in control of 'magical' powers.

A large part of Book IV is lacking in practical significance to the west because the state of kaivalya, the final consummation of yoga training, is not definable in words to those who have never experienced it, and all attempts so to define it have of necessity an unsatisfactory vagueness and intangibility.[1] Hence much of its reasoning necessarily seems inconclusive to us. It is, however, interesting because of the fascinating glimpses it gives of worlds beyond our ken, and of states of being so foreign to us that we scarcely know whether to be attracted or repelled by them; and in that it is a closely woven

[1] Cf. Tennyson, *In Memoriam*, xcv.

> Vague words! but ah, how hard to frame
> In matter-moulded forms of speech,
> Or ev'n for intellect to reach
> Thro' memory that which I became.

logical argument for the existence of the self as an entity has a real importance for western students, more especially as it can be corroborated by recent psychological research.

The question of the existence of a self which is other than the mind is one that has exercised philosophers in the west, and of recent years experimental psychologists have found good evidence for accepting or at least postulating such a self as existent. It would seem that even in the remote ages when the yoga sutras were first formulated it was clearly recognized that the presence of this third factor was likely to be regarded as controversial. The controversy in regard to the self is indeed accepted as perennial because of the definition of ignorance. If ignorance is the underlying mental state of mistaking the temporary for the permanent, the unreal for the real, then from itself arises confusion of mind in regard to the very being of the self. Hence the argument of Patanjali runs as follows:

The self is the basic factor in human consciousness, and freedom from bondage is to be sought in a progressive awareness of the self. This awareness is achieved through a process of withdrawal whereby the self disentangles itself from identity with the mind. It is able to do this because in its inherent nature it is 'constant and not subject to modifications, and is therefore able to observe the modifications of the mind'. The fact that the self can 'cognize the mind as a thing apart' is adduced as a proof of its existence, for that the mind could be aware of itself as an object is untenable. This awareness of the mind as objective to the self is increased by the deliberate identification of the consciousness with the seer rather than with the seen.[1]

For those who are sufficiently interested to seek it, everyday life provides evidence in support of this thesis. We can all by a small amount of introspection become aware of the workings of our mento-emotional nature as of something objective, something other than that which is observing it; and we can to some extent control it. Moreover, most people have had, in moments of material or spiritual emergency, the experience of conscious withdrawal from absorption in the swirl of anxious thought and bewildering emotion into a state of calm impersonal stillness and certainty, which is in fact an identification of the consciousness with the higher self.

There are some to whom the most convincing 'self' experience is that in which at times brief flashes of will direct both mind and body, and such people are often dimly aware that the process is not a mental one. Others have never had this awareness. In them the will works relatively seldom, their

[1] IV. 18–20, 22.

mode of living being almost entirely automatic, for
in the vast majority of human beings at the present
stage of evolution will is an embryonic power and
very little understood. It has, however, of late years
been investigated by various trained experimenters,
and the results, though as yet scanty, are well summarized in Francis Aveling's book *Will and Personality*.[1] Here are described the careful experiments
that have been made in regard to acts of choice and
the volitional experience involved in them, and it
is shown that volition always involves a reference to
self. It must not, however, be assumed that volition
is identical with the yogi conception of purusha or
the self. It is merely one aspect of it, one of the
commonest ways in which it can be experienced.

Having adduced certain proofs for the existence
of the self as apart from the mind, Patanjali goes on
to speak of the true function of the mind as a factor
in consciousness. The mind is a link between the
seer and the seen. It is the lens through which
external objects are registered, and also through
which the seer is enabled to make himself effective
in waking consciousness. 'The mind reacts both to
the seer and to the seen.'[2]

Though the mind has its automatic reactions,
directed thinking is the result of its association with
purusha.[3] Those mental processes which result

[1] Publ. Camb. Univ. Press, 1931.   [2] IV. 23.   [3] IV. 24.

from the stimulation of the mind by the phenomenal world are the most familiar to us, but, as I
have tried to show in preceding chapters, they are
almost wholly automatic. The stroke of the clock
which causes a man to put on his hat and go out to
get lunch, the newspaper headline which recalls to
him such details of the present political or financial
situation as concern him, the crippled beggar in the
street who rouses in him a feeling of pity and makes
his hand go to his pocket—these are the everyday
stimuli that induce the ordinary mental activity
which we often dignify by the name of thought; and
in that they set up a current which repeats itself in
the mind they are exhausting, depleting, a part of
our bondage to the external world. Such automatic thinking tends to dam up the life-force (libido) because it is automatic and repetitive at its own
level and fails to connect the creative self with the
outer world in a real relationship. Analysts have
frequently drawn attention to the fact that such
thought plus the feeling associated with it constitute
one of the commonest defences against actual contact with unpleasant or complex realities. Thus
the man who gives sixpence to the beggar because
of a guilty sense of pity, and then forgets all
about the incident, produces a false but simple
solution to the 'beggar stimulus' which relieves
him of the necessity of doing anything further.

Thought which is creative and refreshing in that it releases energy involves the bringing into harmony of the three factors of the self, the mind, and external phenomena; but this co-ordination does not as yet come easily to the human being, because he has so little awareness of the self factor. Thus if the beggar stimulus is accepted as a challenge to creative action it will induce a consideration of the whole problem of the beggar, to which will be added a recognition of the inadequacy of sixpence as a solution, and all this will necessitate some more adequate reaction—possibly the gift of money together with some kindliness and genuine interest, possibly the withholding of money and reference to an organized source of charitable relief.

It follows that freedom from the limitations of automatic thinking is to be found only in progressive awareness of the purusha. This gradual awareness and predominance of purusha or the spiritual factor in life is slowly achieved by an increasing withdrawal from the external world with which the westerner is so deeply preoccupied. Instead of being involved in the spectacle of living and hence unconscious of one's own identity, it is necessary to become a spectator before whom life unrolls itself as a parchment is unrolled before the eyes of the scholar who seeks to decipher it. From the spectacle as it unfolds wisdom and freedom can be learnt, but not until man is to some extent released from the illusion that he in his essential self is part of the spectacle. 'Then the mind turns from attachment to the external world and is bent toward liberation.'[1]

This state of liberation (kaivalya) which is the true goal of yoga is something far beyond the stage marked by the attainment of the siddhis (supernormal powers). The siddhis are regarded as useful chiefly because they give the student confidence, and are signs to him that he has reached a certain definite stage on his path. But they are also regarded as dangerous. They exercise a fascination and give a great sense of power and achievement, and yet for the yogi to rest satisfied with this achievement is worse than if he had never begun. He has become entrapped in what should be a transitional state, for he has ceased to be an ordinary man and has not attained the godlike state which he set out to reach. Since he is neither god nor man the scheme of things holds no place for him. Nothing short of true kaivalya is a valid consummation.

Now it is obvious to western readers that neither the attainment of the siddhis nor the further attainment of kaivalya which is reached through the practice of unconscious samādhi is a project for the ordinary analyst and analysand. It is as if analyst and yogi followed closely parallel paths up to a

[1] IV. 26.

certain point, but beyond this point the analyst has not as yet ventured. It is clear, however, that analytical therapy is bound gradually to develop some further technique, to enlarge its present boundaries, in order to provide more definite assistance for those who are not content merely to reorganize their present field of consciousness but wish to explore fresh country. It is not possible to say precisely what form this development will take; and no comparison is possible here, for the simple reason that yoga, being a system of extreme antiquity, is a complete thing and has seen and defined its goal, whereas analysis is still in its infancy.

Such tentative experiments as have already been made in the west tend to show that self-determination, self-awareness and creative activity are the gateways to further progress for the individual as for the race. Already there is a conviction abroad that much of our busy 'thinking' is delusory, and is merely a defence-mechanism erected against the fears and insecurities that beset us. We begin to agree with the eastern sage who says that 'the mind is the enemy of the real'. The type of thinking in which the mind revolves on itself is to creative thought as the ordinary photograph is to the painting. The photograph is a mechanical representation of external phenomena, accurate, detailed, useful, but devoid of life; the picture, if it be the work of an artist, is essentially the product of the spirit working through the mind, or rather the mind working in association with the spirit, interpreting and not merely reproducing. The importance of the painting lies not in the object represented nor in the verisimilitude of the rendering, but in the success with which the artist has conveyed the impetus of his spirit. The mind beholds objects, the seer visions.

The technique by which the yogi is trained to a continuous identification of the consciousness with the self, a sustained self-awareness, is in many respects unsuited to western temperaments and western conditions of life. Yet the goal is a worthy one. Freud and his followers have given us, as it were, the first two chapters of our western yoga sutras. It remains for experimenters to discover an applicable equivalent for the remaining chapters.

Chapter XV

THE PROGRESSIVE DEVELOPMENT OF CONSCIOUSNESS

IN a previous chapter[1] I have attempted to give some idea of the fivefold conception of consciousness as it presents itself to the Hindu psychologist, and from time to time throughout this book attention has been drawn to the fact that in the yoga sutras classifications tend to be fivefold because man is regarded as a fivefold being. All five elements or states of consciousness register through the brain, and up to a certain point it is the case that a man's capacity as man depends on the extent to which he can at choice bring these aspects of consciousness into awareness.

At his present stage of development the ordinary human being moves with relative ease in three realms of consciousness, the sensory, the emotional and the lower or concrete mental, and can with training and effort learn to make occasional excursions into higher mental regions, that is regions of insight and creative thinking. In the fifth, that of the self or seer, he has as yet no sure abiding place, and he knows no certain means of entry, although at moments he gets glimpses of the expanded consciousness which is its peculiar characteristic. Such

[1] Ch. VI.

glimpses come through fragmentary experiences of will and intuition. Everyone who has had them recognizes these as being indefinable, subtle, and very elusive,[1] and it is, in fact, much easier and more comfortable to negate them altogether than to examine them, because the brain refuses to register them clearly.

In the west we recognize these five states or aspects of consciousness, but tacitly rather than explicitly; we seldom make the necessary effort to think of them objectively in such a way as to realize our own experience in regard to them. For example, ordinary educated men and women if challenged will admit, as a matter of experience, that their mind functions in two distinct ways, the one an easy and everyday activity that characterizes all waking life, the other a relatively difficult one not always producible at command. When people say 'I cannot make my mind work to-day' they do not mean that the mental automatisms of routine life refuse to function but that another subtler faculty essential for constructive planning and creating is not available. Being unaccustomed to differentiate states of consciousness they use the general term 'mind' to designate anything that is not purely physical. Similarly most people are subject to flashes of intuition, and will admit them if challenged; but few have paused to

[1] Cf. Wordsworth's 'Ode on Intimations of Immortality'.

examine intuition and recognize it as differing in quality, in *kind*, from ordinary mental experience.

In a sense it is true to say that one fundamental difference between eastern and western psychology is that the former habitually and as a matter of course recognizes these layers of consciousness objectively, whereas the latter has hardly as yet begun to differentiate them at all. It would seem that until the existence of a function is clearly recognized it is not possible to evolve a technique for developing it. Hence that these varying functions of consciousness should be apprehended by western psychologists seems vital to future progress.

In the biblical story of man's first beginnings Adam and Eve are described as happy and unaware of the nakedness of their ignorance until they have eaten of the tree of knowledge. At this stage the human mind is incapable of sustained attention, but flits in aimless butterfly fashion from one object to another in response to any external stimulus. To adopt the Patanjali categories, ignorance is here the predominant obstacle, and the acquirement of discrimination is the appropriate discipline.

The next individual or racial stage, that of childhood merging into adolescence, is the one at which the greater part of humanity stands to-day. A mass of sensory impressions have been acquired, the emotions have been awakened and are as yet far more

developed than the mind, consciousness is focused
at the emotional stage and life is lived from the
standpoint of like and dislike. Choice being based
on personal desire and aversion, perception of objective reality is very confused, and a child has
therefore but little judgement or discrimination.
When in Maria Edgeworth's classic tale of *Rosa-
mund and the Purple Jar* the little girl is depicted
as choosing the jar of brightly coloured liquid from
the chemist's window in preference to a pretty pair
of new shoes, we all feel this to be a natural reaction
at the child stage of development. Similarly one
notices that to the immature mind other people
scarcely exist except as objects pleasing or displeas-
ing. When an ordinary child says 'I can't bear Miss
Smith,' he has said all there is to be said about Miss
Smith as far as he is concerned. Hence this stage is
one of fantasy and confused bewilderment in relation to the outer world. Self-awareness is much
greater than at the previous stage, but is still cloudy
and indistinct. The unity that was noted in the first
phase is now a duality, because the focus of consciousness is no longer physical, and yet expression
must still as always be through the physical brain.
The brain is a perfect instrument for expressing
primitive needs, but in proportion as the focus of
interest shifts farther and farther from the purely
physical the means of expressing subtle differences

in experience become less and less adequate, and the sense of duality and conflict grows. According to the yoga sutras, desire is the obstacle, and independence of desire is the discipline.[1]

Although the majority of mankind are still in this second stage, nevertheless an increasing number are passing beyond it. By reason either of inborn capacity or education or both, that which we call intelligence has become highly developed in them, and to a greater or less extent dominates the emotions. Thus the more primitive aspects of like and dislike are renounced for the sake of subtler pleasures, such as those of renown, leadership, learning, philanthropy, and all the pursuits which bring self-approbation in their train. To this group belong scientists, philosophers, all those who do the world's thinking, men of letters, leaders of causes, and so forth. The focus of consciousness in such people is predominantly mental rather than emotional, and there is or may be a clearer sense of the self and a greater control of all the faculties. It should, however, be borne in mind that the phrases here described are selected from an infinite number of gradations merging into one another and relatively indistinguishable. Thus for example it is

---

[1] As explained in Ch. X, although desire and aversion are very commonly taken as opposites, it seems to the writer preferable to include like and dislike as manifestations of desire, and to regard aversion as a slightly different type of obstacle.

possible to recall instances of great statesmen whose consciousness, although they had highly developed minds, was nevertheless focused predominantly in the emotions.

The capacity to use the mind brings with it a great sense of power, and just as in the adolescent phase emotion takes on an unreal and disproportionate value, so at this next stage busy thought expressed in a multiplicity of words becomes all-important and enthralling. The person whose growth is arrested at this point is not free because he is dominated by his own ideas, which tend to express themselves ever more and more mechanically as life goes on. In the phraseology of Patanjali his major obstacle is self-esteem, and he should concern himself with acquiring a true sense of spiritual values. While the bridge between the lower and higher mental faculties has been strengthened, the gulf between the focus of consciousness and the world of physical expression is greater. The sense of duality, of the 'flesh warring against the spirit' reaches a maximum, and ultimately may cause such acute discomfort as to drive the man almost against his will to an exploration of further possibilities of living. But beyond this third stage, that of intellectual focus, the ordinary man does not consciously travel. It is only the relatively few, i.e. few in proportion to the vast numbers of intellectually educated humanity, who are convinced that there are possibilities beyond, and of that number the greater part are aware of inner experience only as it were by accident, and not in the same way as they are aware of thinking and feeling.

The Christian mystic throughout the ages has had his own technique of a very specialized nature for making contact with the spiritual life, and those people to whom the world of mystical religious experience is open usually feel no need for any other means of approach to inner realities. But the world to-day is thronged with people who ardently desire to contact these realities but who for one reason or another are unable to do so through religion as generally understood. This is true not only of the agnostic type, but also of many religiously inclined people who find themselves confused by the formalities and inconsistencies of organized religion, and so turn away from the search for spiritual experience as leading to futility. Modern religion does not stress the search for self-awareness sufficiently to appeal to the scientific or even to the critically intelligent mind. As I have tried to show, one underlying difference between Christian mysticism and yoga is that the latter is psychological and philosophical rather than religious, and hence is of practical interest and value to those for whom religion in the ordinary sense of the word has no appeal.

The method employed by the yogi at this point is self-training of such a nature that the higher and lower mental faculties become consciously co-ordinated. Such co-ordination is effected by the clearing away of obstacles and the simplifying of mental activities, and by subordinating these to deliberate volition in the way propounded in the earlier sutras. The training is undertaken solely in order that the connexion between the two may be firmly and truly established, and that the lower mind may come to be the tranquil mirror of the higher. The figure of reflecting the higher mind in the lower is one very commonly used in eastern psychological treatises, and is self-explanatory to the eastern but by no means so obvious to the western student. Yet it describes what is an everyday experience for us all. As long as the brain is disturbed by the countless ripples of everyday distractions, interiorly generated thought is impossible, because the busy 'brain' does not register its subtle quality as against the dominance and insistence of outer things. Just so ripples break and obscure the image of the mountain and skies reflected in a lake. If the brain consciousness can be rendered calm and free from ripples as a motionless pool of water, then and then only can creative and complete ideas be reflected in its depths without distortion.[1] The effect of

1 Cf. Edward Carpenter, *The Lake of Beauty.*

prolonged samyama is to produce a continuous awareness or alertness of the higher faculties, and to overcome the condition from which we all suffer of being unable to use and control them at will. At the same time the hitherto unrecognized or subliminal activities of will and intuition become more and more conscious and can be used deliberately instead of blindly. It is freedom in being able to cross the bridge between lower and higher modes of consciousness that constitutes the great achievement of the middle period of yoga, and it is an established technique for so doing that is lacking and much needed in the west.

The further stage of kaivalya is not susceptible of description in intelligible terms. Much has been written about it by eastern and western mystics, but all are agreed that it can only be indicated, never defined. Perhaps it may be thought of as a state of unification and awareness at all levels. 'The abiding of the soul in its own nature is kaivalya.'

Chapter XVI

CONCLUSION

THOSE who have followed this attempt at a comparison between the therapeutic psychology of east and west may well ask at this point, What then? Is there any definite practical outcome, or are we dealing with matters of purely academic interest? Is not the attempt that has been made to give the subject an appearance of utility a mere literary device calculated to arouse interest in what might otherwise be too remote to seem real? After all, the number of people in the west who would be prepared seriously to practise yoga as it is practised in the east is infinitesimal; and indeed the climate and general conditions of life in a cool temperate region make its outer observances wellnigh impossible for the European. Is this book another of the many now current which explain at length the nature of our personal (or economic, or social, or political, or religious) difficulties, and either suggest no solution at all, or else one that is so completely impracticable and out of reach that we are left gazing discontentedly into a vacuum?

That yoga in its traditional forms is essentially an eastern practice unsuited to western life and temperament I am prepared to admit. It is true that

playing at yoga has become a fairly common
pastime in certain sections of society, but the relation between this play and the true practice of the
eastern science is comparable to that between the
child who cuts open her sawdust doll to remove its
appendix and the surgeon who actually performs
the operation of appendicectomy.

The ordinary European approach to the idea of
yoga is one that makes any understanding and
utilization of it impossible. Many people have
never heard of it, and that is natural enough. But
among those who attach any meaning at all to the
term, the majority confuse a yogi with a fakir, and
regard yoga as the Hindu science of conjuring and
snake-charming. On the other hand students of
eastern literature who have studied the yoga
writings approach them exactly as a student of
Homer approaches the adventures of Ulysses, or as
a modern critic of the Old Testament regards the
story of Jonah and the whale, i.e. as interesting
folk-lore with at most a symbolical meaning.

Nevertheless, I am convinced that the ideas on
which yoga is based are universally true for mankind, and that we have in the yoga sutras a body of
material which we could investigate and use with
infinite advantage. Here is a method of mento-
emotional training and development used in the
east. It is said on good authority to produce very

remarkable and very desirable results, to open to
the person who practises it new fields of experience,
to give him a poise, an insight, a capacity for enjoyment far beyond anything we have attained.
On the other hand there are countless numbers of
people in the west whose craving for some direct
and real and satisfying experience is intense, who
feel that life must hold the possibility of something
more than they have yet found, and that without
this further possibility it is a hollow sham and not
worth living.

My plea is then that yoga as followed in the east
is a practical method of mind development, quite
as practical as analytical therapy, and far more
practical and closely related to real life than the
average university course. Furthermore, I am convinced that the yoga sutras of Patanjali do really
contain the information that some of the most
advanced psychotherapists of the present day are
ardently seeking. That there is a crying need in
the west for something parallel to this eastern yoga
many to-day would admit. The difficulty is to adapt
the method to current needs without cheapening
the subtleties of real introspective experience on the
one hand, or losing its practical value in a maze
of pseudo-mysticism on the other. This difficulty
should not however be an insuperable one. The key
to the problem lies in a sympathetic appreciation

of the eastern approach to the problems of the interior life. As I have said, this approach is neither atheistic nor superstitious; it is scientific and based upon actual experiment.

Trained to accuracy of observation by generations of scientific research at the physical level, we in the west should be able to produce investigators who would experiment with the statements of writers such as Patanjali, and note the modifications required to suit western intelligence. We need a new kind of Society for Psychical Research, whose aim is not to prove or disprove the existence of poltergeists and spirit-communications from 'the other side', but to demonstrate to the ordinary public the possibility (or impossibility) of genuine superphysical experience on this side. There are many people whose hearts are set on convincing themselves that there is a life beyond the grave. To them their own type of research, and our gratitude to them for the evidence collected by their labours. But there are far more people who are deeply, despairingly concerned to find a greater reality here and now, and it is to them that this book, and especially these concluding words, are addressed.

From my personal experience, small and fragmentary though it be, I am certain that there is a region beyond that painted drop-scene which forms for so many the boundary of this life; and that it is penetrable and susceptible of exploration by those who are sufficiently determined. The path to spiritual reality lies through mental and emotional awareness, and the attainment of this awareness is one of the most subtly difficult and absorbingly worth-while adventures that a human being can undertake. From all quarters to-day we are getting hints and intimations of it—from the modern novelist, the artist, the philosopher, the physicians, the analyst, and the scientist. Each person who has a glimpse of its possibilities attempts to express it in his own terminology, and as yet we have scarcely realized that all are describing aspects of this same truth which is both old and new. For there is a power in the world at such times as the present which evokes a fresh understanding of ancient wisdom, and restates it to meet the need of the age. In yoga and psychotherapy the old and the new converge. From their meeting there may well result an enlargement and intensification of consciousness which will inaugurate a new and more hopeful era for mankind. The east by itself has not achieved it, and the west by itself has so far ignominiously failed to do so. The wisdom and genius of the two combined might accomplish what neither can do alone.

And for those who, like myself, are more deeply interested in what is going to happen here and now than in speculations regarding the future of the race, I would once more reiterate that extension and intensification of consciousness are attainable by the individual who is prepared to pay the price of achieving self-awareness, and that no price is too great to pay for that attainment.

BIBLIOGRAPHY

THE following is a selection of readable books on yoga and kindred subjects:[1]

The Philosophy of Hindu Sādhanā, by Nalini Kanta Brahma. Publ. Kegan Paul.

Psychology and Religion, by Carl Jung. Pub. Yale University Press.

Yoga as Philosophy and Religion, by Surendranath Dasgupta. Publ. Kegan Paul.

Raja Yoga, by Swami Vivekananda. Publ. Kegan Paul.

The Yoga-Sutra of Patanjali, by Manilal Nabhubhai Dvivedi. Publ. Theosophical Publishing House.

An Introduction to Yoga, by Claude Bragdon. Publ. Kegan Paul.   [millan.

An Indian Monk, by Shri Purohit Swami. Publ. Mac-

The Secret of the Golden Flower, by Wilhelm and Jung. Publ. Kegan Paul.

Diagnosis of Man, by Kenneth Walker. Publ. Jonathan Cape.

Modern Man in Search of a Soul, by Carl Jung. Publ. Kegan Paul.

A New Model of the Universe, by P. D. Ouspensky. Publ. Kegan Paul.

The Message of Asia, by Paul Cohen-Porthcim. Publ. Gerald Duckworth & Co., Ltd.

The Hindu View of Life, by S. Radhakrishnan. Publ. Allen & Unwin.

Indian Philosophy, by S. Radhakrishnan. Publ. Allen & Unwin.

The Occult Training of the Hindus, by Ernest Wood. Publ. Ganesh, Madras. English Agents: Luzac & Co., London.

Bhagavad Gita or The Song Celestial (various English translations).

[1] There exist a fairly large number of learned and technical works on yoga written in or translated into the English language, but I do not feel that their titles would constitute an appropriate bibliography to a book of this type.

adg